THE JEWISH HERITAGE SERIES

THE STORY OF THE SYNAGOGUE

THE JEWISH HERITAGE SERIES

THE STORY OF THE SYNAGOGUE

MEYER LEVIN *novelist*

TOBY K. KURZBAND *principal, New York City Public Schools*
Educational Director, Jewish Community Center, White Plains, N. Y.

Art Editor: STEPHEN KRAFT

Illustrations: ROBERT PIOUS

BEHRMAN HOUSE, INC. PUBLISHERS NEW YORK, N. Y.

Acknowledgments

The authors wish to acknowledge the help of many individuals who were influential in developing the ideas and approaches embodied in this book.

To Rabbi Jacob B. Pollak for encouraging the initial experimentation on the course in the Sisterhood Religious Schools and to Dr. Emanuel Gamoran of the Union of American Hebrew Congregations for his help in the publication of a Teacher's Guide, *A Project on the Synagogue* (1945).

To Dr. Alexander Dushkin and to Dr. Jacob S. Golub of the Jewish Education Committee in New York City, for their cooperation with Dr. Gamoran in the Demonstration School at the West End Synagogue and later in a Curriculum Workshop consisting of a dozen participating schools. To Frieda Theaman and to Rose Golub in the Demonstration School, and to Miriam Schmuckler of Temple Israel in New Rochelle, for developing new approaches to the course and new activities for it.

To Rabbi Lawrence W. Schwartz and Rabbi Kenneth E. Stein of the Jewish Community Center of White Plains, New York, and to three outstanding teachers, Nathan Glicksman, Herbert Ferris, and Fae Weiner, who have taught this course continuously in this congregation for ten years before the publication of this book.

To Rabbi Bernard Bamberger and to Dr. Azriel Eisenberg for a critical reading of the manuscript at various times during its preparation and for the many valuable suggestions they made for its improvement.

To Rabbi Morrison D. Bial and to Rabbi Emanuel Green for their painstaking examination of the final manuscript and for their generous contribution of time and energy in this arduous task.

To Rabbi Paul Steinberg, to Rabbi Ario Hyams, and to Frances Long, each for their own special contribution to the book.

And finally, both authors wish to make a special acknowledgment to Jacob Behrman, who acted not only as publisher but as a conscience, a calendar, and time clock, and above all, as a creative artist in his own field, with unbounded patience and with a genuine friendship that sustained us until this book finally saw the light of day.

TOBY K. KURZBAND

MEYER LEVIN

New York, 1957

Foreword to the Teacher

THE STORY OF THE SYNAGOGUE is part of a series to be known as "Our Jewish Heritage," intended for the intermediate grades. Since publication, this volume has been found to be most successful in the fifth grade with equally good results reported in the sixth grade.

The Jewish heritage is the sum of the experiences of the Jewish people from their earliest beginnings which have been recorded in a vast body of literature. From this heritage have been drawn our worship services, our ceremonials, our ethical values, and our religious beliefs. To master all of this heritage would take the work of many lifetimes. Even the greatest of scholars must select specific areas if he wishes to become expert. For children, it is especially important that a selection be made from this vast heritage in such a way that whatever is learned will develop a desire to learn more and to put the fruits of study into practice.

Many studies in educational psychology have indicated that a chronological approach is not the most effective one for children of this age, although it may profitably be used in later grades. Young children learn best when their educational experiences begin with their immediate environment and employ materials that are both meaningful and enjoyable to them. From experiences of this type the children can be led into an appreciation of the Jewish heritage, can have their lives enriched by the significant events and personalities of the past.

To the children in our schools, the synagogue is the most immediate contact with organized Jewish life outside the family. It is here they come to worship on the Sabbath and the festivals, to attend religious school, and frequently to enjoy their recreational activities. The synagogue is also the institution to which their families belong, the one in which each member of the family has his own group associations. In the synagogue, many aspects of Jewish community life find a meeting place.

As the children learn more about their own synagogue and the people who make up their own congregation, they have a key to a very important aspect of the Jewish heritage, the story of Jewish worship. This takes them back to the stories of Abraham and the altar on which he first worshiped the One God. All the great ages of Jewish history and most of the important events and personalities are represented in the story of the synagogue as a house of worship, a house of study, and a house of gathering. The sequence in this book is the product of more than twenty-five years of experimentation by outstanding teachers under the direct supervision of one of the authors. During this time, it has been observed and critically evaluated by some of the outstanding authorities in Jewish education, and their recommendations have added much to its development.

Because the present text has been written by a well-known novelist and gifted storyteller, we hope that it will interest children so that they will enjoy it for its own sake. But we also hope that it will inspire them to do many things to enrich their own lives by taking part in the activities of their own synagogue and by understanding the contribution of the Jewish heritage to these experiences. In an accompanying *Activity Book,* pupils are encouraged to use all their skills and talents to achieve these goals. The *Activity Book* will also serve as a Teacher's Guide to planning classroom experiences for each lesson.

The course on the synagogue out of which this book has grown has been part of a full curriculum for a religious school. It is intended to follow courses in the primary grades on the observance of festivals and on Jewish ethical ideals in the Bible stories. The second book in the series, to follow after the present one, is to be known as *Jewish Ways of Life in Many Lands.* This book will develop the concept of their own Jewish community as it can be experienced by pupils in the intermediate grades and will then compare this concept with Jewish ways of life in Biblical and Talmudic days and throughout the world in our own times. A third volume will carry the story to America and will describe Jewish institutions in this land and the events which have brought the American Jewish community to its present position of leadership.

Now that this textbook is available for a course on the synagogue, it is hoped that teachers will find it easier to teach, especially with the aid of the *Activity Book*. The best textbook, however, is only a beginning. Our fondest hope is that this book will be a stimulus and a challenge to a creative approach to learning so that the synagogue may become a vital and meaningful experience in the lives of our children.

TOBY K. KURZBAND

Contents

UNIT FIVE

How the Synagogue became a house of study

UNIT SIX

How the Synagogue grew and spread to every land

UNIT SEVEN

The Synagogue and you

Maps and Time Lines

For Gabriel, Mikael, Dominique, and Jonathan

For Diana, Paula, and Karen

When do we go to the Synagogue?

CHAPTER I

We start the New Year in the Synagogue

WHEN WE THINK ABOUT being Jews, we think often of the synagogue. This is because the synagogue is the home of Jewish worship and of Jewish studies and meetings and celebrations.

At what times do we go to the synagogue?

Each year, when we begin our classes, we go to the synagogue to observe the most important season of the Jewish year. This season starts with the New Year holiday, called Rosh Hashanah. The whole family joins in the Rosh Hashanah celebration. And the place for the celebration is the synagogue.

The circle of the year

You may wonder why the Jewish New Year comes at the end of summer. Each year is a circle of seasons—summer, fall, winter, and spring. And if we think of each year as a circle, just where does the circle begin? And is the Jewish New Year's Day at the end of summer?

Suppose New Year's Day had to be invented. At what part of the year would you put it? Would you say the year should begin in summer, winter, fall, or spring?

The New Year for others

Some people, like the ancient Romans, thought the year should begin on the shortest day. That day comes in winter. So on that day they would light torches and pray to their gods to give them more daylight. For them, the end of the darkness of winter was the beginning of the new year.

Other people in Europe kept up this Roman custom. They put it in a calendar, called the Roman calendar, which begins the New Year on January 1.

Before the Romans, there were the ancient Egyptians. They did not celebrate the New Year in winter, but in summer. The Egyptians depended on the river Nile to water their land, so food could grow. Every summer the Nile began to rise. So summer meant water and food, and that was the New Year for them.

In ancient Babylon, the New Year began in spring.

And our Jewish New Year begins in fall.

Why did the Jews choose fall?

Let us answer the riddle with another

riddle. When does a day begin? Is it when the sun comes up, or when the sun goes down? Is it in the darkest hour of the night, or at noon when the sun is brightest? We Jews say the next day begins when the sun of this day goes down. We have always said so, for our Bible says, "And there was evening and there was morning, one day." Other people say the day begins when the sun comes up.

So, as you see, these questions can have different answers. And the answer we give shows how we feel about life. There were people in olden times, even long before the Romans, who didn't understand about God. They were afraid in the dark. They were afraid in the cold winter. They were afraid the sun would never come again. So they cried out. They begged for sunshine and for summer, and they tried to make magic.

But the Jews knew God, they knew the sun would always shine again, that summer would always come again. They wanted to thank God for the good things of earth, for the harvest. That is why they made their New Year celebration at the end of the summer. It was because they had no fear—for they knew that God would make the summer come again, that the circle of each year would be the same.

When people think how wonderful it is that the sun will always rise again, that summertime will always come again, that fruit will always grow again, they feel stirred by the beautiful wisdom of God. This is a happy feeling. It is the kind of happy feeling you have on your own birthday, when you want to celebrate together with your family and your dearest friends. And so, on the Jewish New Year, we celebrate the birthday of the world. We celebrate together with our family and our friends and neighbors, in our synagogue.

A time of joy

How do we celebrate? Although the most important part of the celebration is in the synagogue, we make many happy preparations at home. People want to look their best for this great holiday, so they put on their best shoes and best dresses and best suits and coats.

And just as for a birthday, people send out greeting cards with good wishes. The parents make a list of all their friends, and the children lick the envelopes and put on stamps. The greeting card is called "L'Shanah Tova," which means "For a Good Year." Usually it has printed on it, "Wishing You A Happy and Prosperous New Year."

Then comes the big day itself. And

The Romans, Egyptians, and Babylonians celebrate their New Year

you go to the synagogue with your family. For the New Year services, you enter by the big door. At the synagogue, you find all of your friends, grown-ups and children. Everyone is smiling and calling out, "L'Shanah Tova! A happy New Year!"

A time of worship

Why do the Jews celebrate New Year's Day by coming to pray in the synagogue, instead of just having a party or a parade? Because we want to ask God's guidance to lead good lives during the coming year.

In the synagogue all of us take our seats. Our prayer books are open to the services for Rosh Hashanah. Before us, on the platform, is the rabbi. In many synagogues there is also a cantor.

The cantor sings some of the prayers. We all join in part of the singing. Some synagogues have organ music, or other music, just as King David had his harp when he sang and played his prayers to the Lord.

The Holy Ark and the Torah

Then the rabbi turns and faces the Holy Ark. The Holy Ark in each synagogue reminds us of the first Holy Ark in which the Israelites carried the Torah of Moses on their way to the Promised Land. The first Holy Ark was a precious box in which they had put the tablets of the law that Moses brought down from Mount Sinai. And our Holy Ark is also a cabinet, where we keep our copies of the laws of Moses. To remind us that these are the laws God gave Moses, they are copied down

by hand in the ancient way. They are copied on scrolls instead of printed in books. And each scroll is called a Torah, because the Law of Moses is called the Torah.

When the doors of the Ark are opened, there stand the Torahs, in their glittering satin covers, embroidered in gold. They, too, are dressed in their best for the High Holidays.

A Torah is chosen for the reading. Members of the congregation help the rabbi to open the scroll. They remove the Torah's crown of bells, and the silver shield, and the white satin cover. It is an honor to help do this. Sometimes, members of your own family may be given this honor. Sometimes, you may do it.

After the cover is taken off, the fastening that holds the two ends of the scroll together is untied. The two ends of the Torah scroll are rolled apart, opening the Torah for reading.

On Rosh Hashanah, we always read the Torah chapter about Abraham and Isaac, telling how they showed their loving faith in God. And this is why we blow the shofar.

Blowing the shofar

The sound of the shofar is like no other sound in the whole world. The shofar is a ram's horn. It was chosen because long ago our people were shepherds in Israel. The shepherds were scattered on the hills. And when they had to be called together to hear the word of God, they had to be summoned by a sound that carried far over the hills. Since they were shepherds, it was easy for each to

A shepherd blowing his ram's horn

get a ram's horn, for calling and for answering. And the sound of this horn can be heard very far.

In old times the thrilling call of the ram's horn sometimes announced that a prophet of God had chosen a king for Judah and Israel. Sometimes it warned of the approach of an enemy.

Each month, the shofar was blown to announce that the new moon had been seen, for the Jews made their calendar by the moon. And the call for the new moon for the month of Tishri was also the call that announced the New Year. It was the Rosh Hashanah call.

On Rosh Hashanah, the call of the shofar is heard three times. And the sound is something like this: T'keee-yoh!

If you ever try to blow the shofar, you will find that you may nearly burst your cheeks without making a sound come out. To blow the shofar takes practice.

After the blowing of the shofar, the Torah is covered and put back into the Ark.

It is the first day of the New Year, on the ancient Jewish calendar. And the rabbi talks of this. In many synagogues, the rabbi also comes and preaches at a special service for the children.

"L'Shanah Tovah!"

When the services are over, we again wish our friends "L'Shanah Tovah"—"May you have a good and happy New Year."

Now we have seen how the circle of each year, on our ancient Jewish calendar, begins in the fall. It begins with a celebration in the synagogue. We come there to pray, and to hear the shofar, and to ask God to show us the best way to live in the year that is coming. During that year we will come to the synagogue for study, and for worship, and for many celebrations.

THINKING ABOUT WHAT YOU HAVE LEARNED

1. Can you name four ancient peoples who celebrated the New Year at four different seasons during the year?

2. Why do Jews welcome the New Year in the Synagogue?

PARENTS

1. Ask your parents how they celebrated Rosh Hashanah when they were your age.

2. Tell your parents how many children you know in your class and how many of them you just met at the first session.

CHAPTER II

We go to the Synagogue on Special Days

You KNOW THAT WE go to the synagogue to celebrate the Jewish New Year. When else do we go to the synagogue? All through the circle of the year there are regular times, and special times, for coming to the synagogue. There are regular prayers every day for those who wish to come, and there are Sabbath prayers every week, and there are holidays in every part of the year. We also come to the synagogue to study, and for family celebrations such as a bar mitzvah or a confirmation or a wedding. Now let us see about the other important days that are celebrated in the synagogue in the circle of each year.

The day of the new moon

You know that the shofar is blown to announce the New Year. It was also blown every month on the night when the new moon was first seen.

Suppose you were a shepherd long ago. Watching the skies, you would think to yourself, how wonderful is God's world. How the moon grows full, and then disappears, and then grows full again. And you would say, that is a good way to divide the circle of the year. That is a good way to keep the Jewish calendar.

And so our ancestors had watchers on the hilltops, to catch the first glimpse of each new moon, and they would announce the birth of the new moon with a shofar-call. And in the Temple, they had a special service each month in honor of the new moon. And in our synagogues today, we too honor the new moon in our prayers.

Holidays go back to early worship

You may wonder, how did we choose our other important holidays? And were they always the same?

No, they were not. Abraham and Moses did not have the same holidays that we have, because some of the great days that we celebrate, like Purim, had not yet happened in their time. Some of our holidays go far, far back, to Moses and to Abraham, and others are newer. For a people keeps changing, just as a person grows and changes.

You are going to see how worship began, and how it changed and grew until we have our synagogues of today. And perhaps in your own life you will change some things.

But you cannot change what has already happened. And our great Jewish holidays remind us of how our people came to know about God.

Holidays of nature

There are three meanings in our great holidays. Sometimes all three meanings come together on the same day. You will see how this happens.

First, there are the holidays that celebrate nature. These come in the seasons of planting, and of harvest. These are holidays of thanksgiving to the Lord who gave us life, and gives life to plants that grow, and fish and sheep and deer and birds and all the creatures of the earth.

Each time that the crops came up out of the earth, to feed us and to feed all living creatures, our ancestors celebrated the great wonder of life itself. Since they were mostly farmers, they could see this wonder under their own hands, every season.

So we keep the holidays that they made, in the springtime when the earth is ready for seeds. We keep the spring holidays of Passover and Shavuoth. And we keep the holiday of Succoth for the great harvest at the end of summer, when corn is ripe, and when fruit trees are laden with apples, peaches, pears, and other kinds of fruit, and when great bunches of grapes are ripe on the vine.

These are the holidays of nature, the holidays of thanks for health and for the rich joys of living and eating and drinking and feeling the good things of the world.

Holidays of the spirit

Another kind of holiday is the holiday of the spirit. For when our ancestors felt the joy of life they wanted their lives close to God. They felt that God gave plenty for all on this earth, and that all people should learn to live in peace according to God's law.

They felt that the laws God gave them, through Moses, were more wonderful than meat and drink. And these laws kept growing, just as living things keep growing, because in the seed of the Ten Commandments they saw

Harvesting wheat in ancient times

the whole tree of the laws of society.

These laws are in the Torah. And to celebrate God's giving us the Torah, our ancestors took the same springtime holiday, the joyous time of Shavuoth, and they said, "What is more joyful to us even than food and drink?" The answer was "The law! The Torah!" And so they made Shavuoth the holiday that celebrates the giving of the Torah. So you can see how there are two reasons for celebrating Shavuoth.

Holidays celebrating history

There is a third kind of holiday that comes from our history. Such holidays celebrate a great event in our history on earth. But they do not celebrate such days only because we had great victories, or because we were saved. Each time, we celebrate a part of our history in which our forefathers saw the work of God.

Passover is such a holiday. As you know, it celebrates a very great event in our history, our escape from slavery in Egypt. But it also has a greater meaning. For it celebrates the idea that God meant each man to be a free person. It celebrates our belief that even if a person makes mistakes, even if people forget the laws of God, they can learn what is right again, and win their freedom.

Three meanings

So you see that a great holiday like Passover has two meanings. It celebrates a time in our history, but it also celebrates our understanding that God meant us to be free men and not slaves. And it has the third holiday meaning as well. For Passover comes at the time of an old, old shepherd's festival. When the Jews escaped from Egypt, they remembered the old times, the times when they were shepherds in their own land. And they remembered their old festivals. Their freedom came at a time of such a festival, and they made this holiday into Passover.

Esther accuses Haman

Holiday symbols for the circle of the year

So you see how, on some of our greatest holidays, there are three reasons to celebrate: our very ancient customs, in which we thanked God for his beautiful world; our great days in history; and our understanding and love for the life of the spirit.

Another such holiday is Purim. This holiday celebrates the time when Jews were saved from death at the hands of Haman. Long after they escaped from Egypt, some Jews settled in another country, Persia. And there a wicked prince named Haman plotted to have all the Jews killed. But they were saved by a Jewish girl who became Queen, and pleaded with King Ahasuerus to spare her people. As you know, that was Queen Esther. Purim is her holiday.

But you see, Purim is not only the story of a wonderful queen in our history. It has a greater meaning. The meaning is that good must triumph over evil.

Still later in our history, there came a third great event, which we celebrate with a holiday for freedom. This is Hanukah, which comes in the first part of winter.

Passover reminds us of our escape from slavery in Egypt, and Purim reminds us of our escape from death in Persia. Hanukah reminds us of how we freed ourselves from rulers who had conquered us in the land of Judea.

These rulers tried to make the Jews worship idols in their own Temple in Jerusalem. When this happened, the Maccabees rose and drove the invaders out of Palestine. They threw the idols out of the Temple, and purified it, so that Jewish worship could begin again.

So the holiday of the Maccabees celebrates our fight for freedom of religion. Even today, you hear how in some countries people have to fight for the right to worship in their own way. The Jews were the first people to win such a great struggle.

A sad holiday

There are also sad holidays, if you can think of a holiday as sad. For a holy day can also be a memory of a lesson we learned, even though it was painful. One of these sad holidays is Tishah B'Av, which is a date on the Jewish calendar (in the month of Av—on the ninth day). This is the day the Temple was destroyed. And the strange thing is that it was destroyed twice on the same date, although the times were hundreds of years apart.

Once it was destroyed by the Babylonians, who took the Jews into exile. The Jews came back and built the Second Temple. But when they had again grown vain and careless in observing their laws, this Temple was destroyed by the Romans.

To remind us to try to be a better people, this doubly sad day was made a date of fasting, of mourning, and of prayer. It is a very serious holiday.

So you see, our three kinds of holidays have meanings that have sprung out of our past, that have grown from one kind to another, and have become linked together. There are old, old holidays that celebrate the very fact that we are alive and that we have the food and shelter we need in life. And there are the holidays that celebrate the idea that we have been shown how to live together with justice. And there are the holidays that celebrate the great lessons we have learned from our hard times and from our defeats as well as from our victories.

You can see that with all these holidays and services taking place all through the circle of the year, we go to the synagogue all the year round, and that is why many Jews say the synagogue is their second home.

THINKING ABOUT WHAT YOU HAVE LEARNED

1. Which holidays celebrated in the synagogue today remind us that our ancestors were farmers in Palestine long ago.
2. Which synagogue holidays remind us of great events in Jewish History?
3. Which synagogue holidays remind us of the beginnings of Jewish laws?

PARENTS

1. Ask your parents to help you make up 10 word telegrams to send holiday greetings to your friends.

20

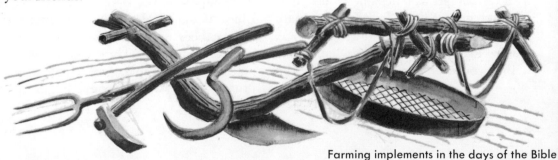

Farming implements in the days of the Bible

What we find in the Synagogue

CHAPTER III

The Torah and Other Special Objects

A visit to the synagogue

NOW THAT YOU KNOW when we come to the synagogue, let us take a closer look around at what is inside the synagogue. For since it is a special kind of place, there is a reason for the way it is built, and for the things that are inside.

At the Rosh Hashanah services you may have noticed some things about the synagogue that you never noticed before. Perhaps you didn't have a chance to ask your parents about them, because when children are taken into the sanctuary of the synagogue during the services, they know they must behave in their best manner, and they must not interrupt the services with their questions. If they do, everybody around them will be saying, ''Sh-hh, Sh-hh,'' and their parents will feel embarrassed.

But in many religious schools a special time is arranged for the classes to visit the sanctuary of the synagogue. Then everything can be looked at closely, and the meaning and use of each object can be explained. Then nobody will say,

''Shh'' if you ask a question. In fact, the more questions asked the better, because sometimes grown-ups think ''everybody knows that,'' when some people really may not have had a chance to find out.

As you first look around, you notice the rows of seats, and the raised platform in front. Sometimes there are two platforms. One of them is for the rabbi and the leaders in worship, and the

22

other is for the Torah Ark. But most often there is one.

Symbols of light

You will notice the Eternal Light before the Ark, and the two large candlesticks on each side of the platform, called Menorahs.

A Menorah has seven branches. The ones in the synagogue may be very tall; they may stand even taller than a man. But you should not think it is wrong if you come into a synagogue and notice only one small Menorah, with not even seven branches. There is no rule about the Menorahs. But it is a custom that has become almost a rule to have such candle-holders in the synagogue. The candle is a symbol of light, and light is the symbol of learning and of faith.

The Menorah also reminds us that our faith has lived for thousands of years, because long before electric lights had been invented, Menorahs were used in our ancient temples to give light.

A service in a Reform synagogue

There is also another symbol of light in the synagogue, and this one is always lit, and this is a rule. It is the light in front of the Ark, and it is called the Ner Tomid, the Eternal Light. "Ner" means "candle," and "tomid" means "forever," or "eternal." Of course, we do not use a candle or even an oil lamp in most synagogues today; we use electricity instead. But the electric lamp that hangs in front of the Ark is usually in the shape of an ancient oil lamp, in order to remind us of the kind that was used in the Temple in Jerusalem. When Judah Maccabee and his followers recaptured the Temple, the first thing they did was to relight the oil lamp with pure oil. This is the story told on Hanukah.

The Eternal Light burns in front of the Ark. You have seen the Ark being opened on Rosh Hashanah, and on other holidays, and on the Sabbath.

Why the Torah is precious

What is so important about the Ark? What is kept inside the Ark?

When you have something precious, you want to protect it by keeping it covered in a safe place. And the more precious it is, the more careful we are about the covering. Precious books and instruments are kept in fine cabinets, which are sometimes decorated in honor of the things inside.

And the most precious thing in the possession of our whole people is the Torah, which is kept in the Ark.

What is a Torah? A Torah is a parchment scroll, handwritten in Hebrew. It is a Hebrew copy of the first five books of the Bible. These books tell the story of creation, they tell the stories of Abraham, Isaac, and Jacob—the story of how our people began. They tell the story of Moses, and they contain the laws that God gave Moses.

Some people have the idea that the Torah is secret and mysterious. But there is nothing secret about it, and there is nothing secret about what is in the Ark. The same Torah, the same history, the same law of Moses are printed in the very same words in every Bible that is printed in Hebrew. And these words are printed in translation in every Bible in English, and in every other language in the world.

Then, you may ask, why don't we just keep a printed Bible in the Ark? The answer is that the scrolls in the Ark remind us of how old our laws are. The Torah scrolls are written by hand, just as they were written in ancient days when these words were first put down. Each scroll is made of pieces of sheepskin, cut and sewn together into a long roll that is wound on two rollers.

That is what books were like, long before printing was invented. And to show that the Law is eternal, our people keep the books of the Law in scrolls of the ancient style.

You may see several Torah scrolls in the Ark. Sometimes they are gifts from people who want their families to be

The Torah opened

remembered in the synagogue. Some of these scrolls are copies made in modern times, but of course exactly according to the old ways. And some are indeed very old, and may have been brought to this country by your great grandparents, or even before.

A Torah must never be destroyed. If it becomes worn out from years of rolling and unrolling, or if the letters fade so that it can no longer be read, it is carefully put away in a special burial place. You may have heard the stories of the wonderful explorations that have been made by archaeologists of today who have found scrolls and other writings that had been sealed away many years ago.

It will help you to understand how precious the Law is if we go back even further, to the time before the Law was written down on scrolls. The Law was not at first written on a scroll. It was on a double tablet of stone. For even before people learned how to write on sheepskins, they wrote by scratching words on tablets of clay or stone. And the Bible tells us that when Moses went up on Mount Sinai to receive the Ten Commandments, he brought them down written on two tablets of stone. This was a very great event for our people and for the people of all the world. Everyone knows that the Ten Commandments are the most important laws, for they tell people how to live together.

The first Ark

The Jews knew at once that these Commandments were their most precious possession. The Bible tells us how skillful artists were chosen to make a beautiful cabinet for the tablets of the Law. This was known as the Ark, and it was carried before the people in all of their wanderings and in all of their battles, on their way to their promised land.

You may wonder why it is called the Ark. Was it, you may ask, anything like a ship, like Noah's Ark? Sometimes words can mean several things. An Ark, in the old days, meant a dwelling place that could be carried. If it was carried on the waters, it was a ship like Noah's Ark. But the dwelling place of the Torah was the Ark that was carried over the desert lands by the tribes of Israel. There is a description of this Ark, in which the tablets were kept, in the Bible. And if you want to know just how it was made, and who made it, and how it was carried, you can read about it in the book of Exodus, chapter 25, verses 10-22, and chapter 37, verses 1-9.

There are many stories about the Ark in the Bible. One of them tells us how it was captured by enemies, and how King David recaptured it and brought it to Jerusalem. David's son, King Solomon, built the First Temple for the Ark. He placed the Ark in the innermost room, known as the Holy of Holies.

So we too, in our temples and synagogues today, have our Ark. But instead of the two tablets of the Law, our

Bezalel directs the making of the Ark

A breastplate, a pointer, and an Ark

Ark contains the scrolls with many laws, which are there to help us follow the Ten Commandments.

To remind us that all of our laws are founded in the Ten Commandments, the doors of the Ark itself are often decorated with a design of the two tablets. And the Ark often has a curtain with a design of the two tablets of Moses, supported by two lions.

The lion was the emblem of the tribe of Judah, who was one of the twelve sons of Jacob. The symbol of each of the twelve tribes is described in the Bible. These twelve emblems are often used as decorations.

The Torah ornaments

When the curtain is drawn aside, and the Ark is opened, you can see that each Torah has a silver breastplate, often in the form of the double tablet of the Ten Commandments. And each Torah has a silver crown, to show that we are ruled

by the Torah. For with the Jews, God's law is the supreme law.

For generations we have loved to listen to the tinkling of the little bells on the Torah crown, and to watch the ceremony when the Torah is taken out of the Ark, for the Law to be read aloud. First the crown is removed and the breastplate is taken off, then the Torah is opened for the reading.

To help the reader keep his place in the scroll, a silver pointer is used. Its Hebrew name is Yad, which means hand, because as you can see it is in the shape of a hand with a pointing finger. These pointers are used because the

Jews always looked upon their Torahs as holy objects, not to be carelessly handled. Often the Yad has beautiful workmanship, with silver threads as delicate as lace.

Showing our love for the house of God

Ever since the first Ark was made to hold the tablets of Moses, our finest craftsmen have tried to make Jewish articles of worship as beautiful as possible. In some of the greater museums in the world, there are collections of silver pointers, breastplates, candelabra, and other objects used in our worship. These articles may be decorated with the Lion of Judah, or with emblems of the other tribes that were named after the sons of Jacob. They may be de-signed with fig leaves, or palm trees, or clusters of grapes, or with other plants. For we like to adorn all that we love. And with this adornment we show our love for the house of God where we come together to worship Him.

You know now that when we come to the synagogue to worship God, the most important thing we find is the Ark, because inside the Ark is the Torah. You know, too, that the story of our people and our first laws are written in the Torah. These are the first five Books of the Bible, and they are inscribed in Hebrew on the scrolls in the Ark.

There are also rules and customs for reading these scrolls in the synagogue. These customs are part of our worship, and you will learn something about them now.

THINKING ABOUT WHAT YOU HAVE LEARNED

1. What is the meaning of the following Hebrew words for objects used in the synagogue: Torah; Oron Kodesh; Menorah; Ner Tomid; Mogen Dovid?
2. Where are the Ten Commandments used in the decoration of your synagogue?

PARENTS

1. The next time you attend services with your parents, point out these objects and tell your parents what you learned about them.
2. Ask your parents to help you make up rhyming definitions of each object.

The tools of the Torah scribe

CHAPTER IV

How we use the Torah

YOU KNOW THAT THE most important object in the synagogue is the Torah. You know that the Torah began with the first tablets of the Law which God gave Moses, and that an Ark was built for these tablets. You know that King David fought to win back the Ark when enemies captured it from the Jews. You know that King David's son, King Solomon, built the First Temple as a safe resting place for the Ark. And that in the same way, we keep writings of the Law in the Ark in each synagogue.

Reading the Torah aloud

You also know that at certain services in the synagogue we open the Ark, take out the Torah, and read aloud the Hebrew words that are written there.

Why do we read from the Torah in this way? And how do we choose what part to read?

As the Torah contains our laws and our history, we read it aloud so that all of our people will know and remember what is written there. And we read certain parts of it each week so that in the circle of the year the whole scroll is read.

A long time ago the Jews realized that the Bible was the most important book in the world. And if you felt that a book was the most important book in the world, how would you make certain that people would read it over and over again? One way would be to have it read out loud, one section at a time. And that is what the Jews decided to do, long ago. They arranged the Torah in portions, so that one portion could be read each Sabbath at the services. There were also special portions to be read on the holidays.

And they worked it out so that there would be portions for every week of the year, and so that the reading would be finished once every year and started over again on the same day. So you see, for hundreds of years the Torah has been read this way throughout the circle of the year.

Simhath Torah

The day on which the reading is finished and started again is a special holiday, called Simhath Torah. *Simha* means a happy time. So the reading of the Torah goes from one *simha* to the next *simha*. It is like reading a favorite story that never ends but begins over and over again, and each time it begins there is a joyous celebration.

To celebrate Simhath Torah, the Torahs are taken out of the Ark and put into the arms of good men of the congregation. Then men march around the synagogue, holding the Torah close to them. In some synagogues they dance with the Torah in their arms, and people kiss the scrolls as they pass, in reverence to God's Law.

From father to son

There is also a custom in which you may soon play a part. For in many synagogues people observe the custom of handing the Torah scroll from grandfather to father to son. This custom was inspired by a story about God and the Torah. When God was ready to give the Torah to the world, he asked the Jews, "What will you pledge for the Torah?" They answered, "We will pledge our children to study the Torah." And this was what God wanted,

for it meant that the Torah would be known and obeyed forever. So the Torah was given to the Jews.

The book of books

This Torah, which is written in our scrolls, is the same as the first part of our big Bible. You know that the Bible is a very long book made up of many short books. It is a book of books.

Since the whole Bible could not be read aloud at services every year, it is this first part, which has our oldest history and our laws, that is read aloud.

This Torah scroll is divided into five books. The beginning tells the story of creation, the story of the first men and women, and of the first Jews. These first Jews are called the Patriarchs because they were the fathers of all the Jews. And so we read the wonderful stories of Abraham, and of his son Isaac, who grew up and had a son named Jacob. Then Jacob had twelve

Simhath Torah in a Conservative synagogue

sons, and, as you know, each one of them became chief of a tribe of Israel.

When there was a famine, they all went to Egypt. And we read the story of Jacob's son Joseph in Egypt, and of how he told the meaning of the dreams of the Pharoah, and how he became Prime Minister. And we read how, long afterward, the Jews were made slaves in Egypt. And we read how Moses was born, and how he led the Jews in their escape from Egypt, and how he gave them God's laws. And then we read these laws, the Ten Commandments, and all the laws that grew out of them. In many synagogues a member of the congregation is called up and given the honor of reading the Torah, or of saying the blessing before and after the reading.

A special privilege

To be called up to do this is a great honor. This custom reminds us that it is really the people to whom the Torah belongs, and the people who make the service. So one of the people is the reader. Sometimes it is an officer of the congregation who is chosen. Sometimes it is a member who has done something special for the congregation. It may be someone who has given a gift to the synagogue. It may be a bridegroom on the Sabbath before or after his marriage. Or it may be a boy who has just had his Bar Mitzvah.

Reading for every occasion

You know that the Torah that we read in the synagogue contains only the first five books of the Bible. These books

A Bar Mitzvah in a Conservative synagogue

together are called the Books of Moses. The other books of the Bible contain the words of the prophets, histories and wise writings and poetry. There are beautiful poems, such as the Song of Songs, and the Psalms of David. For you know King David was famous not only as a fighter, but also for his singing and playing on the harp; many of our most beautiful prayers are Psalms of David.

Together with each Torah portion read on the Sabbath, we also read a portion called the Haftorah, from the books of the prophets.

Other parts of our Bible are also chosen to be read in the synagogue on the Sabbath or on certain holidays. And there are parts in the Bible that are read on the holidays they belong to. For example, the Book of Esther is read on Purim. The Book of Ruth is read in the synagogue on Shavuoth. And the Song of Songs is read on Passover. Ecclesiastes is read on Succoth.

These different books may also be written out on smaller scrolls, and kept in the Ark beside the Torah. Some people love to collect ancient Biblical scrolls, or to give them as gifts. A favorite one is the Book of Esther which makes a lovely, small scroll. One day you may have one, or even make one. Of course you cannot make a real Torah because this is done by special scribes under special rules. But you can imitate a scroll.

The "whole Torah"

All of these books are part of the "whole Torah." Indeed, when some Jews speak of the Torah they mean even more than the Bible. They mean all Jewish learning. For there are famous books written by great scholars, explaining the laws and the stories of the Bible, and these books, too, are spoken of by the Jews as Torah.

There is a saying that when the Torah was given to Moses on Mount Sinai, all the wisdom that was still to come in the world was shown to him in that first part of the Torah. And some people believe that all this wisdom can be found in the Torah of Moses if every word and every letter of every word is examined for all its hidden meanings.

There are many other legends and tales about the Torah. One of these tells us that the Torah existed even before God created the world, and that God looked in the Torah before deciding to create the world.

So you see how important the Jews consider the Torah to be. That is why it is the most sacred object in the synagogue, kept in the most sacred place, the Ark. And that is why we read our people's story, and our first laws, from the Torah during our synagogue services.

But we also read from books of prayer during the services, and you will want to know about them.

THINKING ABOUT WHAT YOU HAVE LEARNED

1. Which holiday celebrates the ending of one year's weekly reading of the Torah and the beginning with the first chapter all over again?
2. When do we read the books of the Prophets at synagogue services?

PARENTS

1. Ask your parents if they will help you make a miniature Torah as described in the Activity Book.
2. Find out what your parents' favorite Bible stories are and which one they would have included in a miniature Torah.

CHAPTER V

How we use the Prayer Book

YOU HAVE SEEN THAT there are many special objects in the synagogue, such as the Eternal Light and the Menorahs and, most important of all, the Ark, with the Torah inside the Ark. You know that we read from the Torah during service. But we also read from another book, and that is the prayer book.

Many prayers are known by heart

The first time you went to the synagogue, you might have wondered how people knew exactly what to say and do. Of course, there was the rabbi to lead them. But do you know that Jews do not always have to have a rabbi to lead the service? Services can even be held without a rabbi. You will learn more about this later on. But each time you go to the synagogue, you see for yourself that many people know the services quite well, and do not have to wait for the rabbi to tell them when to stand up and when to sit down and when to respond in the prayer.

They know, because they know the five books of the Torah very well, and they know their prayer book very well. They know which part of the Torah is going to be read at each service. And they know the most important prayers and songs that will be used at each service, although the rabbi may choose other prayers to add to them.

They know this because everyone who comes to service has a prayer book, and they have been coming to service for many years. Some people bring their prayer books along from home. If you do not bring your own prayer book, then you may have one handed to you at the door of the synagogue, or you may find one at your seat. In this book, we have prayers for every day, prayers for the Sabbath, and for many of the holidays.

Private prayers

Now, there are times when you feel like saying your own prayers in your own words, without a prayer book. In the synagogue, there is usually a time for meditation when each person thinks out his own prayers. And there are many other times, in and out of the synagogue, when a person feels like saying prayers of his very own. It might be the sight of a beautiful sunset that makes you feel that way, or a vast view from a mountain, or being near someone you love, or a cool, quiet moment among trees in a forest. Such moments bring up in you the wish to speak words of awe and praise and joy, to God who created all these beauties of nature. In moments of great happiness a person will feel like singing his thanks for his good fortune, just as David sang and played on his harp. In times of trouble, people often pray for help in words that come from their deepest feelings.

But when people come together to share their prayers in the synagogue, they also want to repeat prayers that bind them together in their faith. They want to share the most beautiful prayers that have inspired Jews all through history. So they read again the prayers that have been most loved, from the Bible, from the sayings of great rabbis, and from religious poems written by great Jewish poets in different centuries and different lands. All of these prayers are in the prayer book.

Prayers throughout our history

Some of our prayers go all the way back to the services in the temple in Jerusalem. Other prayers were written in Babylonia, and others were written in the Middle Ages when the Jews lived in Spain.

There are also prayers that were written in modern times. These are not used in all of our synagogues, because many Jews believe that the services should not be added to, or changed. But others believe that the prayer book is never finished. They believe that while no one can ever add to the Bible, the prayer book may be changed, and that each group of Jews may choose prayers to put into a book if they wish. Of course, even though some new prayers are added, the great prayers of the services are not changed. For many years Jews have agreed which are the best prayers.

Over a thousand years ago, the ancient rabbis began to discuss which prayers belonged in the services. And Rabbi Amram, in Babylonia, was the first one to put together a book of prayers.

The Hebrew name for the prayer book is the Siddur, which means "arrangement." The Siddur arranges the prayers

Rabbi Amram writing his book of prayers

in their proper order.

For centuries, as the Jews moved from Babylonia to Spain, to France, to England and Germany and Russia, they said their prayers in Hebrew. But in each new land they learned the language of the people around them, in order to carry on their daily life. And perhaps, at first at home, they added prayers in the language of their daily life. Now, we have many synagogues where prayers are spoken not only in Hebrew, but also in the language of the country. In our country, we use English as well as Hebrew in most synagogues, although there are many groups who still use only Hebrew in their prayers.

So you see that while the great prayers are the same, not all Jews use exactly the same prayer books. Some groups have special books of prayer for certain holidays. And sometimes the songs come in a separate book, called the Hymnal. The song book may also contain a special service for children.

Prayers for children

Many congregations like to have a separate prayer book for the children's service. In fact, children's services have led to changes in adult services. This happened about a hundred years ago, as a result of the ideas of an unusual man named Israel Jacobson, who lived in Germany and who was a member of a synagogue and a teacher. At that time the services were in Hebrew. And his children, like many others, had not yet learned Hebrew. So when they heard the Hebrew words of prayer they said, ''But what does it mean, father?'' And instead of saying, ''Some day you will know,'' he told them what it meant by translating the prayers. Then he arranged a whole service that the children could understand. It was in the German language. Some older people heard it and said, ''Let us arrange a service that is easier for everybody to understand.'' They called their service ''reformed,'' and the synagogues that used it were the earliest ''Reform'' Synagogues.

Sometimes a class will decide to write its own prayer book. They will select their favorite prayers from the regular prayer book, prayers which they would like to keep in their own book. And then they will select original, new prayers written by pupils in the class, and they will put them in the book. Perhaps you would like to write an original prayer, if your class prepares such a book.

THINKING ABOUT WHAT YOU HAVE LEARNED

1. How many prayers used in your synagogue service do you remember by heart?
2. From what famous book do many of the prayers in our prayerbook come?

PARENTS

1. Ask your parents if they have an old prayerbook which they treasure.
2. Write an original prayer for your family to be recited at some family event.

To whom does the Synagogue belong?

CHAPTER VI

The Synagogue belongs to the Congregation

YOU HAVE LEARNED THE reasons for going to the synagogue and when we go. You have also learned about the holidays and about the daily and weekly times of worship.

And you have seen what is inside the synagogue. You have seen the auditorium and the platform, the Menorahs and the Eternal Light and the Ark, and the Torah inside the Ark. You know how we use the Torah in our worship, and how we use the prayer book in our worship.

Questions to answer a question

Now, perhaps you may wonder to whom does all this belong? There is the synagogue building itself. And there is our religious school. And there is the large auditorium of the synagogue, with the ceremonial objects. And there are all the books.

Does it all belong to the rabbi?

Does it belong to the president, who sometimes sits on the platform with the rabbi?

As you may have noticed, there are sometimes memorial signs on the doors of different rooms, on beautiful windows, or even inside the covers of books. They bear the name of a family or of a loved person who has died. Do these objects belong to the families whose names are on them? Of course you know they don't. All these things are gifts.

Gifts to whom? To the synagogue? But then, we are back at the same question: to whom does the synagogue belong?

Who built it?

Is it like a school, a public building that was built with money from taxes and that belongs to the city?

The members are the congregation

The synagogue is not really like a school. It does not belong to the city. It belongs to the people who belong to the synagogue. That may sound like a riddle to answer a riddle, but it is really very simple.

The people who belong to the synagogue are the members. They are called the congregation. You know that to congregate means to come together, to meet in a group. And so a number of people who come together, who meet in a group to hold worship, are a congregation.

They may be the Jewish people of a town, or of a neighborhood. They may start by meeting in someone's house. And after some time, there may be enough of them in the group so that they want to rent or to build a special place where they may meet for worship.

The congregation builds the synagogue

So it is a group of worshipers, called a congregation, that builds and owns a synagogue. Usually they are people who live quite close together.

When people decide to build a synagogue, does each one own a part of it? No. It is the group, the congregation, that owns the whole synagogue, just as your daily school belongs to all the people who make up your city or town.

But while such schools are paid for by taxes, the synagogue and its religious school are not paid for by regular taxes. Nobody is made to pay for the synagogue. Each member donates as much as he can.

Then of course, after the synagogue is built, there are expenses to keep it in operation. The members pay dues to help with these expenses, and if they can afford it, they give extra gifts for this purpose.

Building a new synagogue

A worship service on the battlefield

The family and the synagogue

From week to week and from day to day, the synagogue is the busy place of your Jewish community. It is even busier than your everyday school.

For parents seldom come to a school, except for a visit. But parents come to the synagogue not only to worship but for many other reasons as well.

They may come, just as you come to the synagogue, to study. In most synagogues there are classes for grown-ups as well as for children. There are always more and more things for Jews to learn about their people, and their religion, and their art, and their books, and their music, if they wish. So there are often classes for grown-ups in Hebrew, and in history and in many other subjects, even in dancing. There are club meetings and gatherings of all kinds. There are lectures, and movies, and Purim parties, and weddings, and concerts, and plays.

But of course the main reason for building a synagogue is so that the people have a place where they can come together and worship. You have seen the building and the ceremonial objects and the books, but even more important are the people who use all these things. For the synagogue is like a house that becomes a home when the family moves into it. The congregation is the family of the synagogue, a big family made up of all the families belonging to the synagogue.

Any ten persons may start such a congregation. In our Jewish law, it is necessary for ten persons to gather together to have a religious service. As one of our earliest rabbis said, wherever ten such people gather together to pray, the spirit of God may be found. And so there may be a religious service on a battlefront, or on board a ship, or in a children's camp or in anyone's home. But when the group grows, they find or build a regular place of worship.

38

The congregation chooses its leaders

Each congregation needs leaders to organize and direct its activities. The members elect a president, a vice-president, a secretary, a treasurer, and a board of trustees. All of these people give their time to the work of the congregation.

Then committees are named to take care of the different activities. There is usually a committee for the school, because the school is most important. There is a committee for the building, a committee for membership, and there may even be a committee to take care of parking problems when children are brought to school.

As the congregation grows, the time soon comes when all the work cannot be done by the leaders in their spare time, and the help of specially trained people is needed. First, the congregation will elect a rabbi to be their spiritual leader, to conduct services, to perform marriages and funeral services, and to work with the religious school and with the classes for grown-ups. The rabbi also does many other things, which you will learn about as we go on.

Then there may be a cantor, who chants, and leads worshippers in singing the musical part of the services. The cantor also officiates at religious ceremonies. Sometimes the cantor is helped by a choir and an organist.

Then the congregation finds a principal to take charge of the religious school, and teachers who are specially trained. There may also be special teachers for the classes for adults in the evening.

And if the congregation becomes quite large, someone is needed to take care of all the business matters. For there may be banquets, lectures, a weekly newspaper, and summer camps to be run. For this the congregation needs a trained executive director and secretaries in the office.

The building itself must be kept in order. Chairs must be arranged and tables put up or taken down. All the ceremonial objects must be placed ready for the services. For this there is a custodian.

All these people together, the officers and the members, the rabbi and his staff, and all the officials, make an active congregation. And it is to all of them that the synagogue belongs, because all of them belong to the synagogue.

THINKING ABOUT WHAT YOU HAVE LEARNED

1. What is the difference between the way money is raised for a synagogue and the way it is raised for a public school?
2. Who are the specially trained people who work full time for your congregation?

PARENTS

1. Ask your parents if they ever took part in any unusual religious services on a boat, in a hotel, in the army, or other place outside a synagogue.
2. Ask your parents to explain how officers are chosen in your congregation.

CHAPTER VII

The Synagogue belongs to You and your Family

THE SYNAGOGUE BELONGS to you and your family, as well as to every other family in the congregation. And if you think of the most important happenings in your life and in the life of your family, you will see that they are a part of belonging to the synagogue.

A place for weddings

Your family really starts in the synagogue, because that is often where people get married. Some synagogues have a special little chapel, aside from the great hall, for small groups of worshippers and also for family affairs. Some have a social hall for weddings and parties.

If the wedding does not actually take place in the synagogue, it may take place at the home of the bride, or in a hotel ballroom, but then the rabbi comes from the synagogue to perform the wedding. And often, too, the bride and groom will visit the rabbi in his study in the synagogue to talk about their future. He gives them advice about how to have a good Jewish home and a

happy family life.

The wedding ceremony is not the same in all synagogues. But in all weddings there are blessings and prayers in Hebrew. And when the wedding ceremony is performed in the home of the bride, or in a ballroom, the rabbi does it as he would do it in the synagogue.

It is also a custom with some congregations for the bridegroom to be called to the platform of the synagogue on the Sabbath before or the Sabbath after

40

his wedding. And there, as you remember, he is given the honor of saying the blessings for the reading of the weekly portion from the Torah. And after the service, everyone congratulates him.

Membership begins at birth

When a child is born to a couple, an announcement of the birth is made at a service in the synagogue. Congratulations to the parents are also printed in the synagogue bulletin. At the next service, the couple may be congratulated from the Bimah. And there 'may also be a beautiful naming ceremony. The child, from birth, is a member of the congregation to which his parents belong.

Some of our modern congregations have nursery schools, so that when a child is four years old, even before he starts attending regular school, he may play in the synagogue's day nursery. He may have holiday parties and sing Sabbath songs and become friends with the little children of other members of the congregation.

Children receive a miniature Torah

When he is a few years older, he will enter the religious school. And this is also a happy time. In some synagogues the new pupil is given a miniature Torah, or a pin with the Ten Commandments written on it. At a special service, called a Consecration, a real Torah is handed from grandfather to father to son. Thus, you see that the Torah is given into your hands, to hand on to your children when you grow up.

Bar Mitzvah and Confirmation

Then, after several years in the religious school, a boy may prepare for his Bar Mitzvah, which takes place when he is thirteen, and in some synagogues a girl may prepare for a Bas Mitzvah. And as you know, the ceremony of the Bar Mitzvah takes place at a service before all the members of the congregation. For the Bar Mitzvah celebrates the time when a boy is ready to become a man, to carry out fully his duties to God.

In many synagogues, there is a confirmation ceremony for boys and girls

The Rabbi performs a wedding ceremony

when they are fifteen or sixteen years old, and at this time they promise to be faithful to Judaism and its teachings.

It is only a few more years after the confirmation that these young people are ready to be married, and they come to the rabbi for advice, and the cycle of life starts all over again.

The cycle of life

You know that this cycle of life is not always easy. Families also have troubles and times of sorrow. There may be a serious illness in the family. Then the rabbi may come to call on the family. Often when people are very sick they want to talk over the inmost feelings of their hearts to someone. And they feel that the rabbi is the one who will listen and comfort them, because he has heard the problems of many people, and he is guided in helping others by the wisdom of our sages.

If there is sickness or other trouble in the family, members of the congregation will often send gifts, or cards of sympathy. And if there is a death in the family, special services are held, and a special prayer called Kaddish is said. Every year, on the anniversary of a death in the family, the memory of this member is kept alive through prayer. This is called Yahrzeit. In some synagogues it is a custom to have a light or a candle burn all day long on the anniversary of a death in the family.

And, as you have seen, the name of the person who has died may be kept alive before the whole congregation by gifts in his memory. There may be a room, or a memorial window, or Me-norahs, or prayer books, or even a Torah, given in memory of a dear one.

Help with daily problems

There are also daily problems in life, and the rabbi is always ready to be helpful in solving them. Sometimes when people quarrel, or disagree, they go to the rabbi to advise them. Sometimes when people cannot make up their minds about such things as a college for their children, or what career their children should follow, they go to the rabbi for advice.

In the old days, even business contracts were arranged and signed before the rabbi. And in the synagogues of the middle ages, there was a custom which made it possible for a man to cry out for justice in front of the whole congregation. If he believed an injustice had been done to him, he was even permitted to interrupt the services in order to tell his side of the story.

Our modern synagogues do not handle problems in exactly the same way, because many problems of justice now belong in the courts of the city and the state. But the synagogue is the place where all the activities of a family in the Jewish community can be carried on. There is some way for every member of the family to participate.

Activities for everyone

The children go to the religious school. The young people have their clubs and their classes and a social program. They may have dances and discussion groups and athletic groups.

Synagogue activities for every member of the family

Parents join the Parent-Teacher Association, which has meetings to help improve the school. They also may join study groups for adults, a dramatic group, an orchestra, or a choral group.

Fathers join the men's club of the temple, which is sometimes known as the Brotherhood. This club may have Sunday breakfast meetings to help raise money for important Jewish work, for hospitals, or for Israel. Sometimes the Brotherhood invites famous people to come to make speeches. And sometimes it gives a party for the ladies.

Mothers join the Sisterhood, which engages in many activities. The mothers arrange charity bazaars. They help with synagogue affairs by serving refreshments. They have study groups, and concerts, and they sometimes have a gift shop in the Temple. Perhaps once a year they have a very big party,

to which they invite the men.

In each of these clubs, you and the members of your family find ways to help the synagogue. And you also find that the synagogue is helping you.

Although all of these activities make the synagogue a very busy place, there are still other activities that center around the synagogue. Your parents may belong to other Jewish organizations which use the synagogue as a meeting place. Some of these organizations help Jews who are sick, or poor, or without homes. Some of them train Jewish refugees for trades and professions. Some of them collect funds to help the Jews of Israel build schools and factories. And there are also Jewish organizations that defend Jews when lies are told about them, or whenever they are attacked. And there are organizations that work for better understanding among people, that try to clear away the lies and superstitions that are spread about any one people.

Understanding our neighbors

Your family probably has friends who belong to other religions. Sometimes people who belong to other religions are invited to come to the synagogue. At these meetings people of different religions come to understand each other. Often they work together to clear up prejudice. And sometimes members of the synagogue will attend meetings for the same purpose at a church. These are all very important tasks. And to help such important work along, members of the congregation may hold special meetings, or raise money to be used for the good of the whole community.

So you see that as you grow up in the synagogue, it becomes a very important part of your world. To prepare for your role in the life of the synagogue, you attend the religious school and the services. You learn all about the importance of the activities of the synagogue, and of worship, and you learn how to take part in all of this. Of course you are interested in all the things your parents do in the synagogue, just as they are interested in everything you do. And sometimes you will discover that you can tell them things you have just learned, or just done, that they too once learned or did but have quite forgotten.

They will be happy to tell you about the things they do in their own groups in the synagogue things you will do when you grow up, and take your own full part in the congregation.

THINKING ABOUT WHAT YOU HAVE LEARNED

1. What are five important events in a persons life which are observed in a synagogue?
2. What are two ceremonies which mark the time when a young person may take his place as an adult in the synagogue service?

PARENTS

1. Ask your parents to describe any events in the life of a person which they have seen in a synagogue ceremony.
2. Tell your parents what "problem" you would like to bring to the Rabbi.

CHAPTER VIII

The Synagogue belongs to your History

WHEN YOU GROW UP AND become a full member of your synagogue, you will discover many things that are new to you. But every time you have a problem, you may ask yourself, and the other members, "Wasn't there something like this, before, in our history?" And you will find that you are helped by knowing what was done before.

History tells us many things

That is not the only reason for knowing history. We want to know history because we are proud of the story of our people. And the nearest part of our history, for you, is the story of your own congregation. From the story of your own congregation you can go back to other congregations in America, and to congregations that your family might have belonged to in other countries before they came to America. You can go back from synagogue to synagogue, and you will see that all the synagogues together may be called "The Synagogue," and that your parents and grandparents and all of your family before them have always belonged to "The Synagogue."

If your own synagogue is a new one, it is probably because you live in a new neighborhood. Then you may ask, who were the first families that came to the neighborhood, and how did they start the synagogue? Where did they live before they came to this place, and what was the synagogue like where they used to live?

If your synagogue is older, you may have noticed in some places in the building the little memorial signs, such as we have already mentioned. Why do people place these memorials to their beloved ones in the synagogue? For two reasons. First they want the family to be remembered in the place that means the most to us in our lives. And, secondly, they want their dear ones to be remembered for the longest time. And the synagogue is the place that will live the longest.

Just as families go way back in history, so do synagogues. Some synagogues have already lived hundreds of years. And just as people have birthdays, so do synagogues. They are called anniversaries.

45

Laying the cornerstone for a new synagogue

Synagogues have birthdays

When a synagogue is young, it may celebrate every anniversary, just as a child does. But as its gets older, members of the synagogue hold special celebrations for the important anniversaries. When the synagogue is twenty-five years old, we celebrate because children have been born and have grown up as members of its congregation. Soon their own children will come to the religious school.

When a synagogue is a hundred years old, it is older than any member of its congregation. It has seen a whole century of life and of history. And yet, with its newest members, it is as young as ever.

Although new synagogues are ''born'' every year, as new Jewish communities are started, there are a good many synagogues in the United States that have had their one hundredth anniversary celebration. In fact, some of them are more than two hundred years old.

Of course you know we do not measure the age of our synagogue by the age of the building, though some of our synagogue buildings are truly ancient. We measure it by the age of the congregation. During the hundreds of years of its life, a congregation may have more than one home, for it is not the house that makes the synagogue, it is the congregation, worshipping in that house.

Congregations have separate histories

And just as a family may move from one house to another, or even from one neighborhood to another, the congregation of a synagogue may move. It may even move from one country to another — right across the ocean! In America you may sometimes find a congregation that is named after a place in Europe. For instance, the Congregation of the Sons of Lublin would be named after a city in far-away Poland. And this may mean that many of the people from that Jewish community in Europe moved to America, and so they organized the same congregation in this country.

One of the oldest congregations in this country was formed by a group of Jews who came from Spain. This is a synagogue that can look back beyond the Revolutionary War. It was already a hundred years old by the time that George Washington became the first President of the United States! It was named Shearith Israel, and it was started by the first Jews who came to New Amsterdam, which is what New York was then called. These Jews arrived in 1654. At first they carried on religious services in their homes. We do not know exactly when they built their first synagogue, but a very early map of New York, which was made in 1682, shows us a small synagogue on Mill Street. So we know it was already there in 1682, which was about a hundred years before the United States was born!

The first synagogues in America

There are five other synagogues in America that took part in the birth of our country. Six sent greetings to George Washington when he became our first President, and the answers which President Washington sent to these congregations are among the most precious treasures in the history of the Jews in the United States.

In his answer to the greetings from the synagogues, President Washington thanked them and told them how happy he was that all men might worship their religion in freedom under the newly established government of the United States. He told them that he hoped Almighty God, whose power and goodness had brought victory to our new nation, would shower His blessings on their congregations.

Another of the six synagogues which sent the greetings was in Newport, Rhode Island. This congregation which began in 1658, built its synagogue in 1763. Their building is the oldest Jewish house of worship still standing in America. For the people of Newport had listened to a famous Christian minister named Roger Williams, who believed that all men should be free to worship God as they wished. In those days not everybody believed this, and even today we have to keep up the struggle to educate people who do not understand the freedom to worship. Roger Williams was one of the first great Americans who struggled for religious freedom, and Jews were glad to find his city free from prejudice.

In fact, when the town leaders of Newport learned that President Washington was going to visit their city, Christians and Jews together met in the Newport synagogue to make plans for the great visit.

It was to Moses Seixas, president of the Newport synagogue, that George Washington wrote his famous, important letter about religious freedom. And this famous old synagogue has now become a national shrine. It is protected by the Government of the United States as an historic building.

The third of the six synagogues which sent greetings to George Washington was Mikveh Israel in Philadelphia, founded in 1740. During the Revolutionary War, when New York was about to be seized by the British, a New York rabbi, Gershon Seixas, took the Torahs to Philadelphia. He is known as the Patriot Rabbi.

CANADA

JESHUATH ISRAEL
Newport, R. I. 1658

SHEARITH ISRAEL
New York, N. Y. 1655

MIKVEH ISRAEL
Philadelphia, Pa. 1740

BETH SHOLOM
Richmond, Va. 1789

ATLANTIC

OCEAN

BETH ELOHIM
Charleston, S. C. 1750

MIKVEH ISRAEL
Savannah, Ga. 1734

EARLIEST SYNAGOGUES IN COLONIAL AMERICA

The settlers in the Georgia territory were helped by the Jewish community of London. In fact, one out of seven of the first settlers in Georgia were Jews. Most of them had come to England from Spain, so they had Spanish names, like DaCosta and DePaz. The very first Jews to arrive brought with them a Torah and Hebrew prayer books as well as Hanukah lamps and other objects to carry on their worship. They opened a synagogue in Savannah and also called their congregation Mikveh Israel. It was organized in 1734.

The congregation of Charleston, was started only a few years later, in 1750. And as there were not a great many Jews in America in those days, the men sometimes traveled far to find Jewish brides. One of the leaders of the Jewish community in Charleston had come from Newport. His name was Isaac Mendes Seixas, and he was a brother of the Patriot Rabbi, Gershom Seixas.

Another of the early southern congregations was in Richmond, Virginia, and it was organized just about at the time that George Washington became president. Some of the very first settlers in Richmond were Jews who traded with the Indians, and who sent out explorers to discover what unknown parts of America were like. One of these was Isaiah Isaacs, a silversmith, who came from England. He formed a partnership with Jacob Cohen, who came from Germany. And one of the people who was sent out to explore new land was the famous Daniel Boone! Daniel Boone surveyed land in Kentucky for Cohen and Isaacs of Richmond.

The congregation in Richmond was started as a result of a Purim party in Mr. Cohen's house. His wife was Queen Esther at this party. And when all the Jews of Richmond got together for Purim, in 1789, they decided to form a congregation called Beth Sholom, "the house of peace and friendship." The copy of the constitution of their group is still to be seen in Richmond, Virginia.

Synagogues spread from town to town

These were the earliest congregations. As the United States grew, its pioneers crossed the mountains and traveled west. Among the first to go into the new places were the Jewish traders. As small trading posts were established, Jews settled in them and helped them to prosper. As soon as a few Jewish families were settled in a new community, they started a synagogue. Thus, in town after town across the United States, synagogues were built. There are few towns and cities in the United States today where a synagogue is not to be found. And if many Jews have settled in a community, there will be more than one synagogue there.

As we have seen, the first meetings of a congregation would be in the homes of some of the members. But as soon as they could, they would build a house of worship. As the town grew, the congregation would enlarge the synagogue or build a new one in a new location. In our larger cities, there are congregations that have moved from one neighborhood to another, in their long history, and lived in three or four different synagogue buildings.

49

A frontier synagogue in early America

The history of your own synagogue

Surely you would like to know the history of your own congregation and its synagogue building. If yours is one of the six that sent greetings to George Washington, then you have already learned in this chapter how old your synagogue is. But if it is not one of the six, then you may still find out its history all by yourself. So, in your activity book, there is a blank space in which you can place a picture of your own synagogue, and under the picture you can write its history.

And this will set you to thinking, where were the synagogues that your family belonged to, long, long ago? Even if your family was among the first who came to America, they arrived only three hundred years ago. We say "only" because the history of the synagogue goes back thousands of years. And the people of that time also belong to our synagogue, and we to theirs. So let us learn how Jewish worship began.

THINKING ABOUT WHAT YOU HAVE LEARNED

1. What record do we have of the first synagogue in America?
2. From which six cities did congregations send greetings to Washington when he was inaugurated as President of the United States?

PARENTS

1. Ask your parents if they remember any celebration or an anniversary of your congregation?
2. Find out from your parents what part your family has played in the history of your congregation.

How the Synagogue started as a house of worship

CHAPTER IX

Judaism began with Abraham and an altar

THE JEWISH PAST OF which we are so proud, and the story of our synagogue, begins with the story of Abraham. For Abraham was the first man to worship one God instead of idols, and it was when Jews began to worship God that they really became Jews.

How did people begin to worship God? Who taught them? Who taught Abraham?

You have a religious school to teach you, and so did your parents, and so did their parents. We know that even the first Jews who came to America started a congregation and a synagogue right away, so that they could gather together to worship God and study the Torah, and so that they could teach their children. These Jews carried the Torah across the Atlantic Ocean, when they came here in sailing vessels. They brought the Torah so that they could not forget what was right and what was wrong in the new strange land.

Before they came to America, they lived in different countries in Europe. And before Jews lived in Europe, they lived on the other side of the Mediterranean Sea, mostly in Palestine, which is now Israel.

Did they have synagogues there?

Not at the very beginning.

You will remember they had a Temple in Jerusalem, their capital. Was the Temple a synagogue? Not exactly. For one thing, it did not have a congregation the way we do. You may say the whole Jewish people was the congregation of the Temple in Jerusalem. But then they could only do what the priests told them. They could not have anything like the congregational activities we have talked about in the last chapters. So you see, the idea of a congregation is something that grew very slowly, over thousands of years. Just as the idea of democracy took a very long time to grow.

You will remember, even before the Jews had a Temple in Jerusalem, they had an Ark which they carried before them. In the Ark were the laws that Moses learned from God.

Abraham was the first Jew

And even before Moses, there were Jews, for hundreds of years. The ones we remember best are the twelve tribes that went out of Egypt with Moses. They were named after the twelve sons of Jacob, the patriarch who came into Egypt from Palestine. And we remember Jacob's father, the patriarch Isaac. And we remember Isaac's father, the patriarch Abraham.

Abraham is called the first Jew. Why? Because Abraham was the first one to say: There is only One God.

Idols, magic, and witchcraft

Did Abraham start a synagogue?

Not like ours. Not even in a tent. Because the people who lived at the time of Abraham worshipped in a different way. These people worshipped idols on altars. And it is very hard to do things differently from the other people around you. They were not trying to find out what was right or wrong. They were trying to do magic, in order to get what they wanted.

For, at first, people thought God was a kind of magic. Some people still do. All the people who lived around the boy Abraham thought they could get things they wanted by begging their idols for them. That is what we call a kind of magic and witchcraft.

They also thought their gods wanted gifts, just as their kings wanted gifts. A gift to the gods was known as a sacrifice. A man would burn a sheep in front of a statue of a god, and he would say, "Look, I gave you this sheep. Now you give me what I want." He might want a large flock of sheep to be born to his ewes. Or he might want an enemy to be killed. If he did not get what he wanted, he would try to pay a bigger bribe to his god. He would sacrifice two sheep, or maybe a cow. Or else he would go and try to sacrifice to another god.

When Abraham was a boy, he lived in the city of Ur. This was in the land that was later called Babylon. And all around him, people worshipped different idols. The biggest idols were for the sun and the moon. Someone would make a statue and say, "This is the god of the sun. The sun is the greatest god because light comes from the sun." Then someone else would make another

Idol worship among the Babylonians

statue and say "This is the goddess of the moon. The moon-goddess is most powerful because she is mysterious!" Then someone else would make a statue of a bull and say the bull is the god of strength. And people would worship the bull, to get strong. Then someone would say, "The god wants food." And they would put their best food in front of these statues.

It may sound to you very much like children playing with dolls. Well, far, far back, grown-ups behaved that way. Some still do. Of course, *you* know that when you are playing with dolls you are only playing with dolls. But you also know how easy it is to imagine that the play is real. And that is what those people imagined.

Sacrifices to idols

And just as children sometimes do cruel things when they are playing, like killing insects and animals, those people in the old days did cruel things because they imagined it pleased their idols.

They would say, "What is the most precious thing we can give to our gods, so they will be good to us in return?" And then they would make gifts of their food, or of their jewels. They would cut up a lamb or a calf, put the meat in front of the idol, and burn it, so that the smell "would be good in his nostrils," for of course the idol could not eat the food.

Their priests were not very different from witch doctors. These priests would examine the insides of the animals sacrificed to the gods. And if they saw any sign of sickness, like spots, or something

54

swollen and black, they would read a fortune from those signs by saying, "The gods are angry." And they would demand more sacrifices.

When the priests and the people were desperate, when there was a time of severe famine, they would do something even more awful. They would even take human beings and kill them and offer them to their gods as sacrifices.

How Abraham found God

Now we wonder how Abraham, who lived among people who did these things, and who was also taught to do these things, was able all by himself to understand that God could not be made of sticks and stones.

Through the ages, rabbis and scholars have thought about Abraham and some of them have given explanations from legends about Abraham as a child. They said that Abraham was the son of an idol-maker named Terach. And since his own father, Terach, made the idols out of clay, Abraham saw that they could not be gods. There is a story of how a very old man came to the shop to buy an idol, and Abraham, who was still a little boy, said, "How can you, an old man with a beard, bow down before an idol that is only a few hours old, because my father just baked this clay in our oven!"

Of course, there had been many children before Abraham who were sons of idol-makers, and who never wondered about this. So if Abraham did wonder when others did not, we see that he was an especially gifted person, even as a child.

Some people are gifted as poets, some are gifted as inventors, some people are gifted as musicians, and there are people with the gift of understanding about God.

Abraham was such a person. All through our history, there have been such gifted persons, who helped the development of our religion. Abraham was the first. When he had grown up, he said, "It is foolish for people to worship so many gods; a god for rain, a god for good harvests, a god for travel, a god for health." He saw that all creation was One, and he said, "There is One God."

Then everyone asked, "What does He look like? Like our sun god? Like a bird or a bull?"

And Abraham could not say what God looked like. For Abraham understood that God was so vast an idea that no man could make a picture out of clay or stone and say "This is God."

The greatest truth

So what Abraham found out, or felt by inspiration, is the basis of the Jewish religion, and of other great religions that have been born since then, such as the Christian and the Moslem religions. Abraham said God is One, and this is what we say when we say Shema Yisrael, "Hear, Oh Israel, the Lord our God, the Lord is One." For this is the watchword of our faith, the first and greatest truth in all creation.

Abraham knew there was One God, but he did not know how to worship Him differently from the people who worshipped many gods. Abraham con-

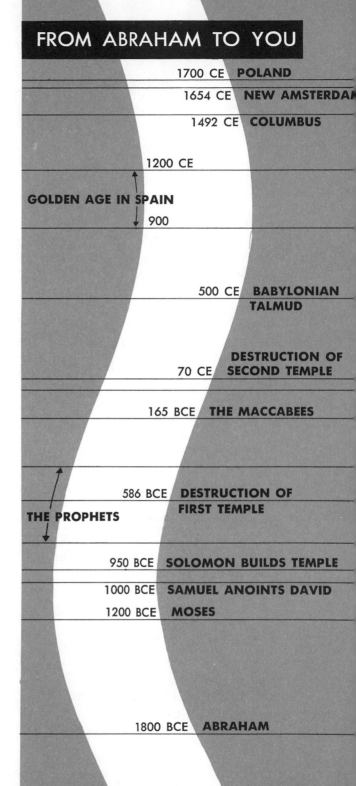

FROM ABRAHAM TO YOU

1700 CE **POLAND**

1654 CE **NEW AMSTERDAM**

1492 CE **COLUMBUS**

1200 CE

GOLDEN AGE IN SPAIN

900

500 CE **BABYLONIAN TALMUD**

DESTRUCTION OF SECOND TEMPLE
70 CE

165 BCE **THE MACCABEES**

586 BCE **DESTRUCTION OF FIRST TEMPLE**

THE PROPHETS

950 BCE **SOLOMON BUILDS TEMPLE**

1000 BCE **SAMUEL ANOINTS DAVID**

1200 BCE **MOSES**

1800 BCE **ABRAHAM**

Abraham leaves the city of Ur

tinued to do some things in the same way that others did. He made an altar of stone, and sacrificed animals upon it. But he would not have a statue that was supposed to be God.

He placed his sacrifice on the plain altar, and spoke to God in the heavens and on earth, because he felt that God was all around him and would know all of his thoughts.

A new land for new worship

The people of Ur, and especially the priests, did not like his new idea. So Abraham had an inspiration from God; God told him to go out from that land, and to seek a new land where he and his family could worship God in their own way. He knew that God would show him that land.

Thus it was that Abraham came to the Land of Canaan, later called Palestine, and Israel. The people in Canaan, the Canaanites, did not have cities like Ur. They were more scattered. They too had their idols and their sacrifices. They sacrificed not only animals, but human beings on their altars. Sometimes they even sacrificed their first born.

It was as though they were saying, "Here, God, I give you life, so you will give me life. I give you what is dearest to me. So don't be angry at me. Do not send thunder and lightning and wild animals.''

Abraham believed that God could not be a trader and make such bargains. And he felt that God could not be a tyrant. He knew God to be good and kind and loving. And he knew that God did not want human sacrifices.

For God showed him this when he told Abraham to take his son Isaac up to an altar on Mount Moriah, and then showed Abraham the ram that was to be sacrificed.

And his son Isaac, and his grandson Jacob, grew up worshipping in the same way. There was as yet no synagogue or temple. A stone altar was their synagogue, and the whole earth and sky was their temple. Each father of a family was the priest, or rabbi. The families were very large, for all the children and their wives and the children's children, and all the servants remained in the big family, or tribe, so long as the old father lived. These great old fathers are called the patriarchs. And the patriarchs Abraham and Isaac and Jacob taught that God was good, and loving, and that He wanted people to be fair to each other, and to be good to strangers. For as God was One, all men were brothers.

Now you know how Judaism began with Abraham. And you will want to learn how Judaism grew, how God's laws were given to the children of Abraham, as all Jews are called.

THINKING ABOUT WHAT YOU HAVE LEARNED

1. Why does the story of Jewish Worship begin with Abraham?
2. How does one of the most important prayers in our service proclaim Abraham's ideas about God?

PARENTS

1. Discuss with your parents how you can include in your allowance the contributions which you make in your religious school class so that you will understand the meaning of ''sacrifice.''
2. Ask your parents for more examples of ''sacrifices'' which grown ups make today.

A Babylonian temple known as a Ziggurat

57

CHAPTER X

How Judaism grew with the Ten Commandments

You know that today a synagogue is made up of many families who come together for study and for worship. And you have seen how in the old days, in the time of Abraham, each family was really part of a great household, called a tribe. The head of this great family was the oldest father, the great-grandfather, whom we call the patriarch. And he was also the leader of worship in the tribe. You have seen, too, how our first patriarch, Abraham, came to know there was One God.

But it took hundreds of years before the children of Abraham, as the Jews are called, were ready to receive God's laws. During those years, they had a great deal of trouble, until they understood that they needed God's laws. And then, another great man of God appeared, to bring the laws to them. His name was Moses. You will see how this happened.

If Abraham had been your father, instead of your great-great-great-great- . . . . . grandfather, you would have grown up and watched him worship God on an altar. He would have told you how he came from a land to the northward, where people worshipped idols, and did not want him to worship the One, invisible God.

And you would meet boys from other tribes. And they would show you their household gods, made of clay or stone. And they would say, "Where is your god?" And you would say, "God is invisible." And they would not understand you.

Perhaps some of your little cousins might think these doll-gods brought good luck. And they would take one home, and hide it, for good luck. And as they grew up, they would still pray to it, in secret, for good luck.

The time of Jacob

That is how it was with the Jews in those days. They were still tempted by all the different people around them, who worshipped idols. For not all of the Jews were as intelligent as the patriarchs, Abraham, and Isaac, and Jacob.

Especially when there were hard times, some of the Jews would try to find good luck charms, and idols. Once there was a very bad famine. There was no rain, and there were no crops, and there was no grass for the sheep or cattle. This was in the time of Jacob.

The Bible tells us how Jacob's favorite son, Joseph, became a slave in Egypt, and how Joseph was so clever that he understood the dreams of the Pharaoh of Egypt. He understood that a dream about seven lean cows meant that a famine was coming to Egypt. So he told the Pharaoh to store up food for seven years, and because he proved to have been right, Joseph was made the Prime Minister.

How the Jews came to Egypt

Then, during the famine, Joseph's own brothers came from Palestine to Egypt to buy some of the food that Joseph had been clever enough to store away. And Joseph recognized them and told them to bring the whole family to Egypt.

That was how the Jews left Palestine and came south to live in Egypt. Each of the twelve sons of Jacob had a family, and so each of the twelve sons gave his name to a tribe.

These twelve tribes of Israel lived in Egypt for years. Their children and their children's children, and their children's children's children tried to remember the One invisible God, but some of them also became superstitious again, and believed in the idols of the Egyptians.

Gradually, the Egyptians forgot that these Hebrews were good people who were descended from Joseph, the clever Prime Minister who had saved Egypt in the time of famine. And they made them slaves.

How Moses saved the Jews

Then Moses arose, to lead the Jews out of Egypt. He told them they must remember their One God, and not believe in many idols. And on Mount Sinai God gave Moses the Ten Commandments.

But while Moses was up on Mount Sinai, many of the Jews began to feel

Egyptians store food in Joseph's time

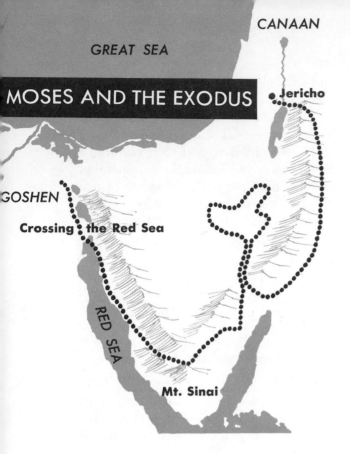

GREAT SEA

CANAAN

MOSES AND THE EXODUS

Jericho

GOSHEN

Crossing the Red Sea

RED SEA

Mt. Sinai

frightened. They saw only the desert around them, and they felt that a miracle had to happen to save them from starvation. Many of them remembered the Egyptian idols. They said, perhaps the Egyptians had the right idea after all. They said, the Egyptians are so powerful—isn't that a sign that their gods are the right ones? They remembered how the Egyptians worshipped a god that looked like a bull, and that was supposed to be a very powerful god.

And so they took all their gold and melted it together to make an idol. This idol was the golden calf

And when Moses came down from Mount Sinai with the two stone tablets, he found the Jews worshipping the idol of the golden calf. He scolded them and

told them that worshipping idols was only witchcraft and superstition. And he explained God's Ten Commandments. The Ten Commandments were not magic. They were laws about how men should live in peace on earth, and how they should worship God.

Nothing so important had happened to the Jews since Abraham. Moses, like Abraham, was a religious genius.

Many generations, and six hundred years, had passed since Abraham discovered the truth of one God. It is easy to understand that such a genius is not born very often.

The Ten Commandments that Moses wrote down were so clear that they are still the main ideas in our laws today.

But it is not very easy to teach people new ideas. There are always some who say the old ways are the best. And so as the Jews continued their wandering in the desert, the grumblers kept saying it was better to worship something you could see, like the image of a lion, or an eagle. An idol of this kind was called a baal, and here and there among the tents of the people, there were those who had their favorite baalim.

Moses designed the first Ark

Moses was wise. He thought that though God cannot be seen His Law can be seen. And so he called together the best artisans, and he had them make a beautiful cabinet. He put the stone tablets into this cabinet, and had it carried in front of the people when they were on the march. Thus, the word of God was carried before them like a flag.

And when they halted, the Ark was

kept in the tabernacle, and the people gathered around it, in a space like a courtyard. And that was how they worshipped the Law.

In this way, we can say that something like a synagogue was born. But is was still very different from the synagogues that we have today.

While the Jews were in the desert, Moses taught the people many other laws that supplemented the Ten Commandments. These were laws about worship, and about health, and about honesty, and about resting on the Sabbath.

Living by God's laws

So you see that the Ten Commandments were the beginning of our Torah. That is why, as you remember, we may have the symbol of the tablets with the Ten Commandments on the front of our Ark, in the synagogue.

We hear in the synagogue how people should live together in justice and according to good rules. In the time of Moses, the Jews would assemble around the Tabernacle to worship, and their laws would be read to them. That was when people first came to understand that the highest ideas in our law come from God, and that the law tells a whole group of people how best to live together.

And so, in their forty years of wandering in the desert, Jews learned more and more how to live as a people under God's laws. The Bible tells us that they were kept in the desert for such a long time because it was hard for the older people to change their ways. And it was the children, who grew up during the years of wandering, who were better able to live by the laws that God gave Moses.

Thus it was the new generation that came into Canaan, to begin a life as a people in their promised land. And it was there that they made a place of worship, the Temple, for the whole people.

You will see how for many years this one place, where the Temple was built, was the center of Jewish worship.

THINKING ABOUT WHAT YOU HAVE LEARNED

1. How does the Bible describe the giving of the Ten Commandments?
2. Why did the Jews make a Golden Calf while Moses was on Mount Sinai?

PARENTS

1. See if you can recite the Ten Commandment by heart for your parents.
2. Ask your parents why they think the Ten Commandments still have meaning for us today even if they are thousands of years old.

CHAPTER XI

How Jews worshipped in the ancient Temple

YOU KNOW THAT JUST as we worship in our synagogue, Jews in all parts of the world worship in their own synagogues. You have also seen that this was not always so. Jewish worship began with Abraham, who built an altar for his great family, wherever he wandered, and wherever he settled with his flocks. But Jewish worship was nearly lost when the Jews became slaves in Egypt. And then Moses led the Jews out of Egypt, and God gave Moses the laws, when the Jews had come as far as Mount Sinai.

Building a homeland

The ten great laws were written on tablets and carried in an Ark, and that was the center of Jewish worship until the Jews came back to the Promised Land.

At last the Jewish people came to the land that had been the homeland of their forefathers from the time of Abraham. The twelve tribes spread out in twelve different parts of the country. But there was only one Ark of the Law, and it remained with the priests as they moved through the land.

This meant that for most of the people the Ark was far away. It was just as though the only real synagogue in America were in Washington, D. C., so that anybody who lived in California or New York or Illinois would have to travel to Washington to attend a real service.

Of course they could worship on their altars at home. But to them this was far from the same thing. As we live today, we know that one synagogue is just as important as another. We know that God is the same everywhere. But in those days they still believed that there was a special power in the priests near the Holy of Holies.

And also, the Jews in the scattered tribes were very busy building their new homes. They had to struggle with other tribes who lived in the same region. It was a long time before all the Jews in Palestine put their strength together to defend themselves and their religion.

The Ark is captured

Again, many years passed before they were united by King Saul, who was anointed by a holy man, the Prophet

Samuel. And then they were attacked by people from another country who came and settled on their seacoast, where Tel Aviv is now. These enemies tried to come up from the seacoast to the mountains, to conquer the Jews, and King Saul fought them. In the battle, the enemies captured the Ark. They took it away with them, imagining that it was a magic thing, and that the Jews would be lost without it. They too believed in witchcraft, and did not realize that God cannot be captured in a piece of stone, no matter how honored and respected it is as a symbol.

After the death of King Saul, David became king, and he defeated the enemy and pushed them back to the seacoast. In his treaty with them, he made them return the Ark. And that was when King David brought the Ark to Jerusalem, singing and dancing in front of it, because he was so happy to have the tablets on which Moses had written God's commandments.

He wanted to build a great temple for the Ark, but the holy men around him, especially the Prophet Nathan, said that David could not build God's temple because he was a man of war who had shed blood. The Ark was kept in a tabernacle outside the walls of the palace, until David's son was king.

The great Temple of King Solomon

This was the son whom he had named Shlomo, which means Peace. And Shlomo, or Solomon as we call him, was the one who built the great Temple in Jerusalem. It had a large outside court for the people and altars for the animal sacrifices, and also an innermost room where the Ark was kept. This was known as the Holy of Holies.

The Temple was the center of the Jewish religion. Was it like a synagogue? It was, and it was not. It was like a

Singing and dancing before the Ark

Building the temple in the days of Solomon

synagogue because it was a place of worship and because the most important ideas and beliefs in our worship were the same as they are today. The belief in God was the same because it can never change. The belief in justice was the same, though our ideas of how to find justice have changed, because the way the people live has changed.

In those days people lived under a king, and the king could decide what was just and fair. Today we live in a democracy, and the people have much more to say about what is just and fair.

The early priests of the Temple

Something like this was true of worship, also. For in those days, worship was conducted by a High Priest and the priests of the Temple. Today we may say that our worship is held in a more demo-

cratic way, since it is the people themselves who make the synagogue and choose their leaders.

When Jewish worship and Jewish law came to the people from Moses, the brother of Moses was made the High Priest, to conduct the worship in the Tabernacle. His name was Aaron. And helpers were chosen for Aaron. All the priests from then on who took care of the ceremonies in the Tabernacle, and later in the Temple, came from certain families. They were known as Cohanim, and even today many Jewish families have the name of Cohen and believe themselves to belong to the families of the priests. In our synagogues we do not have priests, but rabbis, whose work is quite different. And any Jew from any family can become a rabbi.

Then there were people who helped in the ceremonies, who sang, and who took care of many other services. They all came from the tribe of Levi. And today we have many Jews with names that come from the name of this tribe. But today any Jew from any family can help in the synagogue.

When the Temple was built by King Solomon in Jerusalem, there were many beautiful services that were held by the priests, helped by the Levites. We can read about some of these services in the Bible.

At that time, the Jews did not celebrate all of the holidays that we do today, for some of the events that have given rise to our holidays had not yet happened in the time of the First Temple.

But three of the great holidays that they celebrated were Passover, and Shavuoth, and Succoth. Three times a year, all those who could do so made the pilgrimage to Jerusalem, bringing their gifts to the Temple.

As you remember, some of our great holidays were also festivals of nature, celebrations of planting and celebrations of the first crops of the early summer. For in Palestine, which is a warm country, there is more than one crop each year. Then in fall, there were festivals for the crops and the fruits at the time of Succoth.

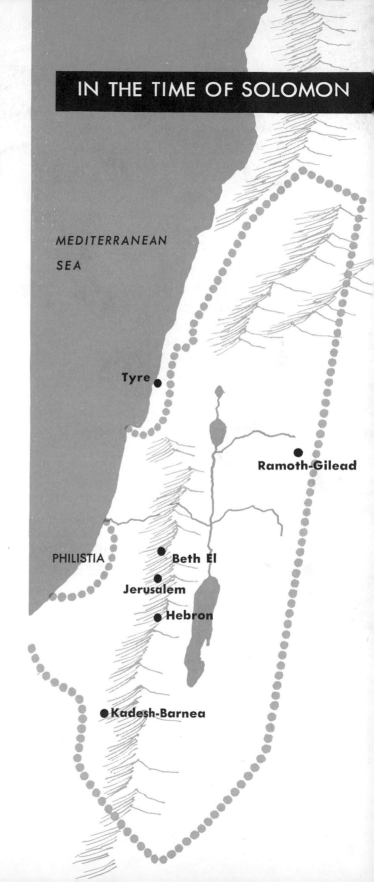

IN THE TIME OF SOLOMON

MEDITERRANEAN SEA

Tyre

Ramoth-Gilead

PHILISTIA

Beth El

Jerusalem

Hebron

Kadesh-Barnea

People traveled far to worship

You can imagine the people coming a long way to worship, and therefore making a great holiday of their trip. You can imagine entire families, and sometimes entire villages, filling the roads on their way to Jerusalem. They came with their donkeys loaded with first fruits, and they led their prize sheep and even their cattle as gifts for the Temple.

There would be singing on the way, singing on all the roads, singing of the Hallel, the joyous thanksgiving songs to God. They sang the songs of David, and other beautiful prayer-songs and poems, such as have come down to us in the Psalms. Some of the poorer people may have brought their only sheep to be sacrificed.

When they reached the city, the people slept in the fields or in tents, and on the holiday itself they crowded into the Temple courtyard, to watch the priests make the sacrifices.

The sacrifices were a custom that had survived from far back in the past, and that was still practiced by the Moabites and Jebusites and other tribes who lived all around them. But Jews knew that the real idea of our religion was to worship God to find out right from wrong. Moses had given them the first laws that showed right from wrong.

The time of the prophets

And now, prophets were speaking the words of God, to show what was good and what was bad. Who were these prophets? Were they the high priests? Or were they other priests, who took care of the worship in the Temple? They did not have to be priests. They are known as men of God, men who, like Abraham and Moses, had the gift of understanding the will of God.

You have already heard the name of one of these gifted men, the Prophet Nathan, who came before King David and told him that he could not build the Temple because he was not a man of peace. Now you will learn something of these prophets, and how they helped the growth of Judaism.

THINKING ABOUT WHAT YOU HAVE LEARNED

1. What are the most important ways in which the ancient Temple differs from our modern synagogue?
2. Which holidays were celebrated by pilgrimages to the Temple?

PARENTS

1. Ask your parents what their favorite music is in the worship service and why music is an important part of the service.
2. Invite your father and mother to help you make plans for the building of a model temple.

CHAPTER XII

From Temple to Synagogue: the Prophets show the way

You know that as a baby grows up, it takes a long time for the baby to learn what is right and what is wrong. The same thing is true about a whole nation. And the same thing was true of the Jewish people when it was young.

They had the Ten Commandments from Moses. They had many other laws of worship given by Moses and the priests. They came to the Temple in Jerusalem, bringing gifts. But in daily life many new things happened, and people could not always be sure what was right and what was wrong. They could ask the king to judge, and if he were a wise king, like Solomon, they could believe in his judgment. But there had been wicked kings, too, and kings who had broken the Ten Commandments. Who was to judge the kings?

The prophets spoke in judgment

There were wise and holy men, called prophets, who could speak in judgment on kings. They were men who did not want riches or power. The people could see that these men wanted only to find out what was good and right. There was something in the hearts of the prophets that said that winning wars is not the surest way to prove what is right. Building a magnificent temple is not the surest way to prove what is right. Building a magnificent temple is not the surest way to prove you abide by God's law. A prophet could even come before a king and tell him, "You have done wrong." The prophets had no authority, as Abraham had over his great family, or as Moses had over all the Jews who escaped from Egypt. But they brought the word of God about what was right.

How did a man become a prophet?

He spoke out before people, telling them God's word. Sometimes these men would predict things that were going to happen, and if their predictions came true, they became even more famous.

But they did not make predictions like magicians or fortune-tellers. They made predictions from what they saw was happening. If they saw that people were wicked, they predicted that these people 67 would be punished. We would also say that the prophets were inspired.

What is an inspiration? It is an idea that comes to someone, that comes so strongly that he feels he has to make it known to the world. Perhaps it is a feeling about how beautiful the world is, a feeling he can express in a poem, or a piece of music, or a painting. Perhaps it is an inspiration to preach about the goodness of God's world.

A prophet in Israel was a man who was inspired by God to bring messages to the people about what was right. He felt that he spoke God's words. Sometimes the prophets said that terrible things would happen to the people if they disobeyed God's words. They said the people would lose wars and become slaves, and that Jerusalem would be destroyed and burned.

Who were the prophets?

A long time has passed since the time of the prophets of the Bible. We have their words, written down in the Bible, and we have stories about them, so we know what sort of people they were.

First of all they were men who tried to show that they did not want anything for themselves. Some of them wandered about in rags, and lived on very little food. The Prophet Elijah, who was one of the first we know about, went out into the desert so he could be by himself and think clearly, listening for the voice of inspiration from God.

These prophets, when they felt inspired, would go before the people and speak out. A prophet would stand in the marketplace of a village, and people would gather around him as he told them what he thought of the way they were behaving, or even of the way the king was behaving.

And if what he said seemed sensible, and people agreed with him, he could cause changes to be made. We have several stories in the Bible of prophets who went right up to a king and accused him of sin.

Even King David quailed when he did a bad thing, and Nathan the Prophet came and stood before him and told

him so. You know the story about how King David sent a captain into the thick of battle so that he would be killed and his wife made a widow, because King David wanted to marry her. That was a terrible thing for him to do, and Nathan the Prophet told him so. The King was ashamed, and the people were angry with him. The words of Nathan the Prophet have come down as a lesson to us to this very day. Even now books are written about it, and a movie was made about it, to remind people not to do such wrongs.

In our own time, we don't have prophets exactly, but we do have people who believe very strongly that they can tell what is right. Sometimes such people become famous preachers. Sometimes they become famous writers or radio or television commentators who speak out and tell high officers of the government when they have done something wrong.

And of course the rabbis and the ministers in places of worship are following in the way of the ancient prophets when they speak out about what is right and what is wrong.

One of the early prophets was Amos, who told the Jews that God did not want their worship if their hearts were not pure, and if they did evil to their fellow men.

Another of these ancient prophets was Jeremiah. He even used ideas that remind us of our own advertising methods. When he wanted to warn the Jews that if they kept on doing wrong, Jersualem would be captured, and they would all become slaves, he thought of a way to show them what he meant. He took a big wooden yoke, of the kind that were put on oxen when they plowed the fields. And Jeremiah put this yoke around his own shoulders and walked around Jerusalem that way, to show the people they would become slaves, like oxen, unless they obeyed God's laws.

A warning fulfilled

A conqueror had already come from the North, had conquered the tribes that lived furthest from Jerusalem, and had taken them away into captivity. Thus, ten of the tribes of Israel were gone, and they became known as the Ten Lost Tribes. Even today we do not know what became of them.

But still the people of Jerusalem would not listen to the prophets. And, just as Jeremiah had predicted, the King of Babylonia came. He destroyed the Temple that Solomon had built, and took the people away from their homes. He forced them to march all the way across the desert to Babylonia. Whole families had to make the march.

Jeremiah warns his people with the yoke of an ox

WHERE THE PROPHETS LIVED

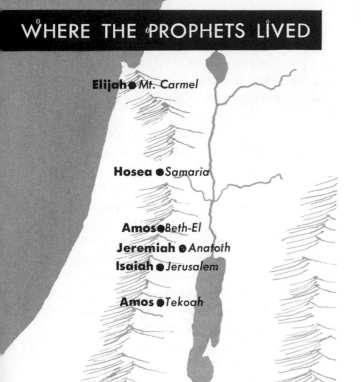

Elijah● Mt. Carmel

Hosea ●Samaria

Amos●Beth-El
Jeremiah ●Anatoth
Isaiah ● Jerusalem

Amos ●Tekoah

After this they remembered how the prophets had told them they would be punished for having sinned and forgotten their God. Then they knew that Jeremiah had been right, and they wanted to repent. They wanted to worship, but they were being driven far away, and their Temple in Jerusalem had been destroyed.

Defeat and exile

The Babylonian soldiers who were guarding them along the way laughed at them and said, "Where is your great Hebrew God that we heard so much about? Our God is more powerful than yours, because we beat you and destroyed your Temple."

For the soldiers of Babylonia were still like children, and to them a god was only a magic charm, in a war. They had names for their gods, Marduk, and Ishtar, and Nana, just as in the old days when Abraham had lived in those far countries. The Babylonians still had not learned the truth of one God. And now they demanded of the Jews, "What is the name of your God?"

The Jews said his name could not even be spoken, because they began to understand that God is beyond all human understanding. They said, "We have no name for him, except He Is."

And they knew that their prophets had spoken the word of God, and they had been defeated, and their Temple had been destroyed, not in any contest of gods, but because of their own wrongdoing, their own greed. And so even in their defeat, they recognized the truth, because once again they began to understand about God.

And as they struggled toward Babylonia, they wanted to worship. They were homesick for the sight of their Temple on the mountain of Jerusalem.

A march of sorrow

When people have deep feelings, ordinary words are not enough for them. They cry out their sorrow, and their sorrow becomes a song. It is the same, too, when they have great joy. Their joy becomes a song.

This march was a march of sorrow, and they cried out. Some of them repeated the words of the Prophet Jeremiah, and they repeated them so much that at last they were written down, and they have come to us in the Bible:

My heart is sick within me
O that my head were water
And my eyes a fountain of tears
I would weep day and night.

And others kept remembering the terrible sight of Jerusalem being burned, of their homes being torn down, and of the people being driven out of the city until nobody lived there. Some of their words of mourning are in the Book of Lamentations in the Bible:

How does the city sit alone
That was full of people.
How has she become as a widow
She that was great among nations
And a princess among the cities
How has she become a slave.

And so at last they came to Babylon. One thing they tried to do was to stay together. Some of the priests who had come with them tried to comfort them. Even if the people had been wicked, the priests said, now they were punished, and God would forgive them if they obeyed His laws.

A prophet named Isaiah arose and spoke of times of peace, when nations would beat their swords into plowshares. Today mankind is still striving for this peace, and the United Nations has the words of Isaiah on its walls.

One day, this prophet told the Jews, they would return from Babylon, as their ancestors had returned from Egypt. And they would rebuild the Temple. The main thing was not to forget, not to forget all the laws they had learned since the time of Moses, all the laws that were in the Holy of Holies in Jerusalem.

"If I Forget Thee, O Jerusalem"

So the people swore not to forget. They swore it in a great poem, which is in the Bible:

If I forget thee, O Jerusalem,
Let my right hand forget its cunning
Let my tongue cleave to the roof of
my mouth
If I remember thee not.

This was a very great oath. Because it did not mean only forgetting the city of Jerusalem. The city of Jerusalem stood for the Temple, and their laws, and God. So it meant:

If I forget the ways of God, then let my hands forget how to do their work, and if I forget the word of God, then let my tongue stick to the roof of my mouth so that I cannot speak any words at all.

You can see how strongly they felt. Their words were so true to Jewish hearts that they have come down to us to this day. We still use these words

The destruction of Jerusalem

when we want to vow that we will not forget the needs of our people, that we will remember the laws which show us what is right and what is wrong. "If I forget thee, O Jerusalem."

Then after they had sworn not to forget, they had many discussions about how to remember the Jewish laws and the worship of God.

Because, as we have seen, when they lived in Palestine, the Temple was their way not to forget. The visits to the Temple and the sacrifices in the Temple made them remember the laws. Even so, many people had slipped, and disobeyed the laws.

Now, without the Temple, what could they do to help them remember?

This problem made them sad, and even frightened them. And this is the poem they repeated about their feelings:

By the rivers of Babylon
There we sat down, yea, we wept,
When we remembered Zion.
How shall we sing the Lord's song
In a foreign land?

And they did not forget

The last question was their real problem. How to sing the Lord's song, how to say the Lord's words, how to remember the Lord's laws. For you know, too, that if people have no synagogue to go to, if they do not attend worship, they may forget the laws of God.

But, you will say, they can read the laws in the Bible.

And that is the answer that was found in Babylon. The people talked about their problems with the priests. One of the wisest was Ezekiel, who had been a priest in the Temple. A priest, too, could speak as a prophet. Just like Jeremiah, he had prophesied that the Temple would be destroyed if the Jews again worshipped idols. So the people turned to Ezekiel and asked him, "What will happen to us?" He did not say, "I told you so." He said, "There is hope." For the priests and the scribes had thought of a way to worship without the Ark, without the Temple. God's words could be remembered and written down.

THINKING ABOUT WHAT YOU HAVE LEARNED

1. How does our word "conscience" help us to understand what the prophets called a "still small voice" of God?

2. How can we explain today what people meant when they said that the prophets predicted the future?

PARENTS

1. Ask your parents how they have helped you to know right from wrong. Do they remember any time when the lesson was not an easy one?

2. Is there any person living today whom your parents would look upon as a modern "prophet"?

CHAPTER XIII

How the Synagogue may have begun in Babylon

IN SOME THINGS A PEOPLE grows little by little, just as a child grows. At first a child cannot speak, but can only express its feeling with cries and laughter. Then we learn to talk. And still later we learn to write down our thoughts.

And so when Abraham first knew God, he hardly knew how to express himself. He worshipped on an altar of stone. And as the Jewish people grew in their understanding, there came Moses who received God's word in the Ten Commandments. Then the people worshipped in a tabernacle. And later, instead of a tabernacle, they built the Temple.

All the while the priests and the prophets were trying to help the people understand God's laws. The priests conducted the services in the Temple. The prophets thought deeply about the laws, and spoke the word of God in the market place. Finally, the words of the prophets were written down.

How the laws of Moses were saved

When the Temple was destroyed, the Laws of Moses were saved because they were remembered and written down, and the words of the prophets were written down. But the Jews asked, where could they worship without a Temple?

The earliest synagogues

We find that later they had begun to worship in synagogues. We do not yet know exactly when or where the synagogues began. We are still finding out many things about our past, through excavations and discoveries of records. Perhaps when you grow up there will be discoveries that will tell us exactly when the first synagogues began.

But up to now we believe that synagogues began in Babylonia, after the Jews had lost the Temple in Jerusalem. We do know that there were places of worship and places of study very much like the synagogue among the Jews of Babylon, and we think they may perhaps have begun with the priest-prophet Ezekiel.

How did they begin? A way was needed to keep the Jewish faith alive. We know that Ezekiel wished for this so 73 much that he dreamed about it.

Did you ever wish very hard that something would happen, and then have a dream about it? When the Jews were forced to live in a strange land, in Babylon, they wished they could be home in Palestine.

Ezekiel's dream

Ezekiel had a dream. And this dream is told in the Bible, for the Bible tells us many stories based on dreams. It tells us how Joseph became the Prime Minister of Egypt because he interpreted the Pharaoh's dreams.

And so Ezekiel told his dreams to the people in exile. In his dream, he said, God sent him to a valley that was filled with dry bones. "A valley of dry bones?" the people thought. They were living in a valley. And weren't their

hearts dead? So they felt as though their lives had become nothing but dry bones. So the dream was about them.

Ezekiel told them more about his dream. God had commanded him to speak to the dry bones, and they would join together again and rise up as human beings. Then, in his dream, as he spoke God's words, the miracle happened, and the bones rose up and were a multitude of people.

And just so, Ezekiel told the discouraged Jews, they too would rise up again. Because the word of God could come to them in this land as well as in their own land. Had not God spoken to Abraham in this very land, to show him the way to Palestine? And had not God given Moses the Ten Commandments in the dry wilderness of Sinai?

God was everywhere. He was One, and He was everywhere, since He was God of all the world and all creation. It was not only in Jerusalem that He could be worshipped. He could be worshipped wherever people found themselves.

But how? the people asked. How could they worship here when their

Ezekiel dreams of a valley of dry bones

holy place, their altar, and their Holy Ark, was in Jerusalem?

But what did they worship? they then asked themselves. Was it not God's law?

That was when the wonderful idea to write down all their laws, as the priests remembered them, came to the people in exile. Perhaps they already had a few scrolls, containing parts of the Law. But now they wanted to write down all their laws, so that no matter how they were scattered, they could have the Law that was the center of their worship. Each group could carry their scrolls of the Law. And many scholars today believe that this idea was the birth of the synagogue.

You may think it was a very simple idea. But when people are used to doing things in a certain way, it is very hard for them to change.

If your school burned down and all the books were burned, the teachers would gather you together in a different place, perhaps in someone's home, and they would tell you the lessons from memory until they had new books.

That was what the priests and the scribes did in Babylonia. Not all the Jews were in one city. In fact, they were scattered in many places. Not every group had a priest from the Temple among them. But there were scribes, called soferim, who could copy the scrolls.

And if there were not enough priests, then the people could gather together with the scribes and study the scrolls, so that every man understood the laws. And this gathering together to hear the laws was like what we still do in the synagogue.

The scribes were very important

In those days not everybody could write. Nowadays, it would be simple, because everyone could copy the Bible, or, of course, get a printed Bible, because the Bible is the most popular book in the world. There are more copies of it than of any other book that ever was written. But if it were not for those very first scribes who copied it by hand, letter by letter, always exactly alike, we wouldn't have the Bible today, with its wonderful stories, and with our history, and with the laws of Moses.

As you know, they copied it down on pieces of sheepskin, that would last practically forever. But, you may ask, who decided what should be written down and put into the Bible?

Some parts had already been written down, by priests and their scribes. Other parts had been memorized, and handed on from priest to priest. These were then written down. We do not yet know exactly when and how it was decided 75 which books should be kept in the Bible. It was long after the Jews came to Babylon that this work was finished, for the Bible tells us of their life in Babylon and of the return to Jerusalem, and of much that happened after that. During those hundreds of years scribes, or Soferim, were at work. Soferim were very learned men; they were experts in our history and our laws, and they became the teachers. And during this time Jews began to see that it was more important to listen to the Law than to make sacrifices on an altar. Thus the priests, who made the sacrifices when the Temple was rebuilt, became less important. You did not have to be a priest or be born a Cohen to study Torah. And any learned men could discuss God's Law. Then, in our history, we begin to hear about rabbis, who were learned teachers.

From those first days of the exile in Babylon, the priests and the scribes and the people themselves had discussed which books were the most important to us.

Beginning with the creation

If you wrote the story of your life you would start when you were born. And so the Bible starts with the story of creation, as their fathers had told it to them, and their father's fathers, all the way back to Abraham, and Noah, and Adam.

After telling the stories of Adam and Eve, and of Noah, and of all the fathers and sons, they wrote down the story of Abraham, because he was the first Jew, the first man to understand that

there was only one God. They wrote down the stories of his sons and grandsons, and how they came to understand what was right and what was wrong. They wrote down the story of how Abraham's great-great-grandchildren went to Egypt and how their great-great-grandchildren were slaves, and how Moses freed them and gave them the Ten Commandments.

Together in a strange land

One of these Commandments, as you know, is to keep the Sabbath a day of rest. Because God made the world in six days and rested on the seventh.

And on the day of rest, it was natural for families to come together, especially as they were strangers living in a strange land. The old people would tell the old, old stories, the Bible stories. Several families would gather together with the priests, and the stories and the laws would be read from the scrolls, and they would sing.

Thus, the Jews of ancient Babylonia found the answer to the question of how they could sing the Lord's song in a strange land.

They could sing it in Sabbath worship, among themselves.

And their priests reminded them of the important days of worship when they had gone up to the Temple in Jerusalem. Those were the holidays when they brought their fruits and their sheep to be offered in thanksgiving sacrifices. They had done this on Passover, and Shavuoth, and Succoth.

They had given thanks on Passover, because God freed them from slavery.

Ezra reading the scrolls before the congregation

They had given thanks to Shavuoth, because God gave them the Ten Commandments.

They had given thanks on Succoth, for the fruit of the earth.

And so now, in Babylon, on these same holidays, they read the stories of those times from the scrolls. And these stories gave them hope that the Jews would once more be freed, and once more return to Palestine.

Thus, in every place where Jewish families gathered, they read the scrolls, and each place became a substitute for the Temple. Each group became like a congregation.

We do not know whether they had special buildings where they gathered for this kind of worship. Most likely they did not, for the scribes would have written about those houses of worship.

Food for thought and belief

As you know, the main thing in our worship is the Torah, and not the building around it. And that is what the Jews discovered in Babylon. They found out that even if the Temple had been torn down, even if they had been driven to a foreign land, the Torah remained.

And so they began to think and to study and to discuss things about the Torah. It was no longer as it had been in Jerusalem when the High Priest could decide the meaning of the Law. Since they had been driven out, and scattered, and since some of the important priests had escaped to the other side of Palestine, to Egypt, no one could really have the power to decide about the Law. The priests and the scribes and the holy men who were called prophets all told their ideas about the Torah, just as our learned rabbis help us to understand the Torah today, just as the learned judges help us to understand the Constitution and the laws of the government.

For example, one of the Torah sayings that puzzled the people in Babylon was that children should be punished for the wrongdoings of their parents. Should laws follow the idea in this saying? 77

There was a saying, "The fathers have eaten sour grapes, and the children's teeth shall be set on edge."

Now, many people make mistakes, or are wicked, and it does not seem fair that their children should be punished for it. Some Jews thought perhaps the saying meant that if parents are bad people, their children will be bad. But this also did not seem to be fair, or always true. The Jews of Babylon were especially worried about this, because they knew that the prophets had blamed the older people for their sins in Jerusalem. The prophets had said that was why the Jews were beaten, and driven out of their homes. Now, was the new generation, in Babylon, also to suffer for those sins?

The Prophet Ezekiel told them this could not be God's meaning. He said that the children would be punished only if they repeated the sins of their fathers. Each person could learn what was right and what was wrong. God would judge each person according to his own behavior.

And thus, on their day of rest on Sabbath, they talked about the real meaning of the Bible sayings, and of their Law. And they told each other the newest words of the holy men who had risen in Babylon.

How Isaiah brought new hope

One of these new prophets was named Isaiah. He is called the Second Isaiah because there had already been a prophet of the same name, in Jerusalem.

During the time of the Second Isaiah, in Babylon, a wonderful thing happened for the Jews. They were no longer

Isaiah announces the end of the exile

prisoners in Babylon. For a conqueror had conquered their conquerors! A king named Cyrus had come from Persia and conquered Babylonia! And Cyrus was good to the Jews in Babylonia. He said they could go home to Jerusalem and rebuild their Temple.

When this news came, Isaiah spoke out. And he said some very important things. He said that God didn't give us our freedom, and give us His laws only for ourselves. He said that all the world, all men, ought to know that there is only One God. All men ought to pray to One God. "For My house shall be a house of prayer for all peoples." And Isaiah put this new thought into a great poem, about going back to Jerusalem and building the new Temple.

"It is too slight a thing
Merely to gather the tribes of Jacob again
And restore the children of Israel.
I will also make you a light to the nations
That my salvation may reach to the ends of the earth."

And that proved a true prophecy, for the people of all nations look upon the Ten Commandments and the Bible as a light for all mankind.

THINKING ABOUT WHAT YOU HAVE LEARNED

1. Why did the Jews in Ezekiel's time have to find a new way to worship God?
2. Is there any way in which the words of the Bible have become a "light to the nations" as the second Isaiah prophesied that they would be?

PARENTS

1. Ask your parents which man in our country today gives people hope and courage?
2. How do your parents feel about the idea that children are punished for the "sins of the fathers"? and about Ezekiel's answer to this idea?

The palaces of Nebuchadnezzar — King of Babylon

CHAPTER XIV

A Synagogue at the gates of Jerusalem

PERHAPS YOU HAVE HEARD your parents talking about how Jews from many lands are going back to live in Israel. And they may have spoken of a few countries whose rulers do not allow Jews to leave. That is the way it was in the ancient days when the Jews lived in Egypt and were not allowed to leave. And for fifty years when they were in Babylonia they were not allowed to leave. So you can see how happy they were when the new ruler said, "The Jews can go."

Ezra the scribe

One of the people who wrote down the story of those days was Ezra the Scribe. He was also a priest, and there is a whole book of his history in the Bible, called the Book of Ezra. He starts by telling us about his own ancestors, tracing his ancestors the way people did in those days by saying, *"Ezra,*
the son of Seaiah,
the son of Hilkiah
the son of Shallum
the son of Zadok
the son of Ahitub," and he goes
on all the way to Eleazer the son of Aaron, the high priest and brother of Moses. So you see he was an important man from an important family.

Ezra tells us how the new Babylonian ruler, Cyrus, told the Jews they could go back to Jerusalem and build their Temple. Cyrus even said they could take along all their silver and gold, so they could buy bullocks and lambs for sacrifices, and use the rest of the money to do whatever their God bid them.

A long walk homeward

Then Ezra tells us exactly how many people went back from Babylon. He says 42,360 people made a big caravan, with 7,336 servants, and "they had two hundred singing men and singing women." He even wrote down that they had 736 horses and 435 camels and 6,720 donkeys. So you can see that most of them walked.

Thanks to Ezra, we have this exact information about what our forefathers did, so many hundreds of years ago!

Not all the Jews left Babylon. Many remained there, because they had homes and businesses, and Jews were not badly treated. They sent gold and silver to help rebuild the Temple in Jerusalem, just as many Jews send money to help build Israel today.

A few years after Ezra counted the numbers in the first group that left for Palestine, other groups left, and Ezra the Scribe went with one of them. He tells us how his caravan crossed a great river, and came into bandit country. They prayed that they might not be attacked by robbers. And finally, after walking for four months, they came to Jerusalem. Ezra had brought along his scrolls of the Bible.

So you see, when the first Jew—Abraham—came to Palestine, it was with the idea that worshipping idols was wrong, and there was

ONE GOD.

Then after the Jews went to Egypt and became slaves, Moses brought them back to Palestine, and it was with the

THE TORAH.

And after they were conquered and taken to Babylon, Ezra the Scribe came back to Palestine with the

SCROLLS OF THE BIBLE.

Rebuilding Jerusalem

But it was a sad city and a sad country that Ezra and his followers saw, when they at last came to Jerusalem. The wounds of war and destruction had not been healed. Most of the country was barren and laid waste, and it was hard for the returning Jews to earn a living.

It was as it was in modern times when the first Zionists went back to Palestine and found the country a barren waste again. They had to clear swamps and plant trees before a living could be earned.

In Ezra's days, the first thing the people had to do was to rebuild the walls of Jerusalem. Otherwise they could be raided by fierce tribes of Ammonites, and made slaves.

The walls of Jerusalem had been torn down when the Jews were conquered by the Babylonians. And they had never been rebuilt. You could see the burnt part of the great gates, hanging from their huge hinges.

Rebuilding the walls of Jerusalem

Ezra and his followers had a hard time settling in the war-torn land. They found that many Jews who had come in the great first caravan had mingled with the tribes of the Samaritans. Many young men among the adventurous first settlers had married the daughters of non-Jewish tribes. And their children were being brought up to speak strange languages and to worship the idols of those tribes.

An open-air synagogue

But when these people heard that the great Scribe, Ezra, had come from Babylonia, they were reminded of the Book of God's Law, and they returned to Jewish ways. There was a place where many people gathered; it was the water gate down in the valley. People went there daily to fill their jars. And one day, at the gate in the broken, old walls, people cried out, "Let Ezra bring the book of the Law of Moses, the book which the Lord commanded to Israel!"

And Ezra brought out the scrolls which he had carried from Babylonia, and he read from early morning until noon, with all the men and women standing and listening to the Law of God.

He did this every day. Soon they built a wooden platform, there by the water gate. The Bible tells about this, as clearly as though we could see it happening today. "Ezra opened the book in the sight of all the people, for he was above all the people, and when he opened it, all the people stood up. And Ezra blessed the Lord, the one true God. And all the people answered

Nehemiah freeing the Jewish slaves

Amen, Amen, lifting up their hands. Then they fell down before the Lord, with their faces to the ground." And Ezra and other priests read in the book, from the Law of God, distinctly, and they gave the sense of what they read, and explained it so that everyone could understand.

So, you see that was a kind of open-air synagogue, before the gates of Jerusalem.

Nehemiah came in a time of need

When the Jews came back from Babylonia to build the Second Temple, they needed help. And so they sent back messengers to Babylonia, just as nowadays messengers come to us from Israel to tell us of the help they need.

One of these messengers went to a very important Jew who had done good

82

work for a certain King Artaxerxes, whose palace was in Shushan. This is the same Persian palace where Queen Esther saved the Jews.

And the visitor from Jerusalem spoke with the important Jew, whose name was Nehemiah. Nehemiah asked, "How are things going in Jerusalem?"

"Pretty badly," said the messenger. "The city walls are still torn down and we are at the mercy of raiders."

Nehemiah became worried. "How is Ezra the Scribe?" he asked.

"Ezra has helped the people, but life is still too hard for them. Even if they want to follow God's Law, they find it hard."

Nehemiah could think of nothing but this sad report. He decided to go before his king and ask for leave to depart to help the Jews in Jerusalem. He waited until the king was drinking wine and in a good mood. Then he told his story.

And the king not only said that he could go; the king said Nehemiah would be the Governor of Jerusalem. And he gave him a letter to prove he was Governor.

How could this far-off king make somebody Governor of Jerusalem? Well, you remember the Babylonians conquered Jerusalem, and so whoever ruled over Babylonia still ruled over Jerusalem, although it was far away.

83

Perhaps Nehemiah convinced the king that it would be a good idea to help the Jews rebuild their city and their country, for if the Jews had greater wealth, they would pay more taxes to the king.

Nehemiah came to Jerusalem without telling anyone. He spent a few days riding around and inspecting the ruins and deciding what was to be done. Then he called a meeting of the richer men, because even in a poor city there are some who are well-to-do. He showed them the letter making him Governor. And he said, "Let's start all over." For one thing, he said, all those men who had Jewish slaves should free them.

Times had been so bad that many poor Jews had had to sell their farms and then they had sold their daughters, and at last they had sold themselves into slavery. Now Nehemiah told their masters, "It is a shame for a rich Jew to have poor Jews as slaves." And because he was the new Governor, and because Ezra the Scribe helped in his plea, the Jews decided to free poor Jews from their debts, and to start all over.

A Golden Book of helpers

Then Ezra called for volunteers to build up the walls of Jerusalem. And he wrote down a roll of honor of all those who came and worked on the walls. You can see that even today everyone who reads the Bible can read the names of those Jews, so it was certainly a lasting honor and a great reward. It is like the Golden Book today, where the names are recorded of Jews who give money and help to build the synagogue. There is also a Golden Book in Jerusalem today, with the names of Jews from all over the world who helped Israel.

First, Ezra's volunteers built up the many gates in the walls. They built the fountain gate, and the sheep gate, and the fish gate, leading to the markets. Then they built the walls between the gates. The good work took fifty days, with everybody, even the women, helping out.

At first their enemies laughed at their work, saying "What they build a fox can tear down." But when the walls were finished, people moved into the city. Nehemiah lent them money to build houses, and Jerusalem became strong.

The Temple and worship are reborn

Then the services at the Temple were important again. More and more people came from all over the country for the festivals.

They held a big Succoth feast. And again Jews came to Jerusalem for the holidays, three times a year. Those who could not come to Jerusalem celebrated at home in their villages.

Nehemiah put the whole country in order and divided it up into districts. There were twenty-four districts. In each district the people gathered together in what was called the House of the People. We do not know if this was exactly a synagogue, but it was, we know, also called the Meeting Place of God.

And in these meeting places they read from the Scrolls. They recited the same prayers that were said at the great services in Jerusalem.

So the team of Ezra and Nehemiah had done great work when they came back from Babylonia. They had started Jewish communities into something like the kind of life we know today. It is no wonder that the story of their work, in turn, was later written down in the Bible. The Bible has a whole book about each of them, so they are honored and remembered forever.

THINKING ABOUT WHAT YOU HAVE LEARNED

1. How did Ezra feel about Jews in Palestine who had married Samaritans and what did he want to do about it?
2. Why is the story of the Platform at the Water gate in Jerusalem looked upon as an early synagogue?

PARENTS

1. Are there any people whom your parents could suggest for your synagogue's "roll of honor"?
2. Is there any important synagogue event coming for which your parents would like you to make posters?

Musical instruments used in the Temple

CHAPTER XV

How the Maccabees saved Jewish worship

It was jewish worship and Jewish study that had kept the Jews together even while they lived in exile in Babylonia. As they no longer had their Temple, they started reading the law in meeting places that were like our synagogues. When they returned from exile to Jerusalem, and built the Temple again, those who lived in villages and on farms away from Jerusalem made meeting places near their homes. In these gathering places they could listen to the word of God read to them from the scriptures.

Thus it was that Jewish worship and Jewish law were preserved for many years.

A time of peaceful growth

After the Jews returned from Babylonia and rebuilt the Temple, there was a time of peace. Again Jewish children were born and raised in Judea. They learned how to watch the sheep, and to become farmers, and how to make things out of leather and wool. And they went with their fathers to the

Meeting Place of God, to worship. The most honored of all the children were those who learned to read and write, and studied the scrolls. Some became scribes and teachers.

During all this time the Jews were not a free people. Their country was still ruled by Persia, since the Persian King Cyrus had conquered Babylon. Taxes were collected and taken to the rulers of that foreign land.

But the Jews did not mind much. Fathers told their children that as long as they were free to worship the One God, they were satisfied. Because no king could be as important as God. Kings died, but God was forever. Kings could be conquered, but God was all-powerful.

A conqueror from the north

And it happened just as they said, that the faraway king of Persia was conquered. Another King had come from the north, a young warrior whose name you may already have heard, because it is one of the most famous names in the history of the world. His name was Alexander the Great.

Alexander the Great came from the lands we now call Greece. And he marched his armies through Syria and conquered Babylon and all of Persia, so that in the end, he governed all the countries that Persia once had owned.

Among these was the little Jewish country of Palestine. Alexander the Great even came to Palestine. But he did not start a war there, because the Jews did not resist him. They would just as soon pay taxes to Alexander as to the King of Persia, so long as they were left in peace to worship God.

And Alexander understood this. When he came to Jerusalem he was very respectful of the High Priest of the Temple. Instead of riding into the city on his horse like a great conqueror, and making the priest bow down before him, Alexander got off his horse and walked on foot and knelt before the High Priest.

A dream that saved the Temple

This was because of a dream. You remember how important dreams were to the people in those times. There is a story that Alexander was marching across Palestine to attack Egypt, when he dreamed that the Jewish High Priest showed him how to win a battle. So Alexander was thankful, and he showed respect for the High Priest when he passed through Judea. His army had to pass that way because the land of Israel has always been a road between two rich kingdoms. To the north were Babylonia and Syria. To the south was the way to Egypt. All the conquerors

Alexander the Great

who wanted to capture these kingdoms had to make a road through Palestine. And sometimes they fought their battles on this road.

It is as though you lived in a small house between two fighting neighbors. First the Egyptians had gone north to conquer the Assyrians and Babylonians. Then, after hundreds of years, the Babylonians were the strong ones, and they came south through Israel and Judea so that they could get at the Egyptians. Then the Egyptians again became strong and went up and drove out the Babylonians. But they ruined Judea on their way. And when Judea was rebuilt, down came Alexander, and Egypt was conquered again. Alexander became ruler of all of these lands, north and south. He was king of the whole civilized world of those days. And he died young. Some say he was bored because he had no more worlds to conquer. 87

Judea passed from hand to hand

When Alexander died, the same thing happened that often happens when a very rich man dies. His relatives and friends quarrel over his wealth. So Alexander's generals quarreled, and divided up his kingdom.

One general said, "Egypt is for me." Another general said, "I'll take Syria." They kept on dividing and quarreling. Judea was passed from one to another. And that was how the Jews got a new ruler. He was a Greek, like Alexander, and he came from Syria, which was then ruled by the Greeks. And for many years he didn't bother the Jews in their religion. He simply appointed some of the Jews to collect taxes for him, and these Jews became rich.

You know how people like to imitate their rulers. The rich Jews who were working for the Greek rulers tried to behave just like the Greeks. They imitated the way the Greeks dressed, and

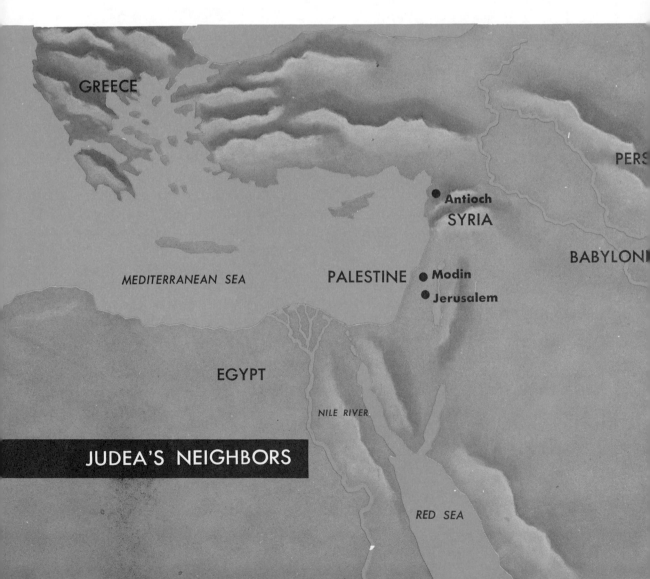

GREECE

PERS

Antioch

SYRIA

BABYLON

MEDITERRANEAN SEA

PALESTINE ● Modin

● Jerusalem

EGYPT

NILE RIVER

JUDEA'S NEIGHBORS

RED SEA

they spoke the Greek language as though it were more fashionable than Hebrew.

Many Greek officials and traders came to live in Palestine, and they showed the Jews the Greek way of life. They practiced the famous Greek sports like discus throwing, they built gymnasiums and theaters, they had horse racing, and they drank a great deal of wine.

They also brought their own kind of books, which were different from the Jewish books. The Jewish books were about God's Law, but the Greeks had story-books and myths about their many gods. And soon the old struggle began, between the One God and the idols of the many gods. Not that the educated Greeks of those days really believed in their gods. But they regarded them as symbols, and they wanted the people they ruled over to accept their gods as a sign of bowing to their rule.

Some Jews thought it was fashionable and more fun to behave like the Greeks and to worship the Greek gods like Zeus and Hermes and Aphrodite. And so the Jews were divided. There were those who wanted to forget their religion and behave like Greeks, and there were those who wanted to be good Jews.

The rule of the mad King Antiochus

Finally, one of these kings who ruled Judea from Syria decided that all the Jews should be forced to behave like Greeks. He knew that the Jews had always been allowed to worship in their own way, in their Temple. But this king, whose name was Antiochus, and who was called a madman, ordered his soldiers to put a statue of Zeus in the Temple, and he ordered the Jewish priests to make sacrifices to it, and the Jews to bow down to it. The Greek soldiers thought it was great fun to force the Jews to eat forbidden foods.

Jews who refused to behave like the Greeks were often tortured and killed. You know the story of brave Hannah and her seven sons. The soldiers ordered her family to bow down and worship their gods. Each son said no, and was killed, and Hannah was proud of them, and she died by her own hand.

This story makes us feel very angry, and it had the same effect on our ancestors. It made them want to fight. But they had no weapons, as the rulers forbade Jews to make weapons.

The Bravery of Mattathias

There was a good old Jew, a priest named Mattathias, who had five sons. They lived a day's walk from Jerusalem, in the town of Modin. One day the soldiers came to Modin to set up an altar to Zeus in the market place. They ordered all the people of Modin to come and bow before it. And because Mattathias was the elder of the town, they ordered him to be the first to bow to the idol.

Mattathias refused. But one of the town Jews who liked to imitate the Greeks said, "I'll be glad to do it." But before this Jew could bow down, Mattathias struck him and killed him. Then the five sons of Mattathias rushed upon the soldiers, and killed them all. Now the people of Modin knew that trouble would come. Old Mattathias 89

Weapons of the Maccabean army

called out, "Whoever is for the Lord, follow me!" Thus, the war began with a call to religious freedom.

Revolt against the Greeks

Hundreds of the best men followed the old priest to the hills. They hid in caves. They began to make forbidden weapons of iron. And from other towns, Jewish fighters came. Soon there were many bands of fighting men in the caves. They proudly remembered their Jewish history, for these were some of the same caves where King David and his bands had hidden out. From these caves, they could make raids on the enemy.

Judah Maccabee leads the Jews

Judah, the son of Mattathias, was the leader of the raids. He sent out scouts to watch when troops of the Syrian army were coming along the roads. And when the soldiers camped at night, the Jews would attack them, and then melt away in the darkness.

Soon Judah had several thousand men in his units. And he was given a nickname. He was called "The Hammerer" because of the way he hit the enemy.

The conquering Jews became known as Maccabees. And you know even today we have clubs and sport teams named after the Maccabees.

Soon the Syrians sent a big army to find the Jewish raiders who were fighting for religious freedom. The army sent by King Antiochus was so large that they felt sure that even half of them could destroy the Jews. So the other half stayed in camp as reserves.

The night before the Syrians expected to start their battle, Judah and his men slipped out of their camp, leaving torches burning to fool the Syrians. And Judah made a surprise attack on the Syrian reserves. Even though the Maccabees were outnumbered ten to one, they beat the surprised Syrians.

The other half of the Syrian army did not know this had happened. They spent the whole day in the hills hunting for the Maccabees. And then they marched back to their camp, very tired. And that was where they found Judah, because he had captured their own camp and was waiting for them. So this half of the Syrian army, too, was surprised, and Judah and his Maccabees beat them and drove them all the way back to Syria.

Mad King Antiochus was very angry, and started gathering an even larger army to beat the Maccabees. The war went on for many years. Three times the Syrians sent armies to beat Judah and his Maccabees. Four of the five brothers, sons of the priest Mattathias, died in these battles. But in the end, the Syrians gave up. They withdrew their armies from Palestine, and the Jews were free again, in their own land. Free as they had not been since the days of King Solomon's sons.

Freedom to Worship

The Maccabees had won the war for religious freedom. It was the first time in the history of the world that a people fought for the right to worship as they pleased. Those were our people.

The Maccabees captured the Temple in Jerusalem, and cleaned the idols out of the holy places. You know the story of how they searched for pure oil to light the Menorah. And how they found only a small portion of oil, but it burned for eight days until new oil could be prepared. That is why we have the custom of lighting candles for eight

Cleaning the Temple after the Maccabean victory

days on the Feast of the Maccabees, called Hanukah. The word Hanukah means "the dedication," for they cleansed and dedicated the Temple.

The last of the hero sons of Mattathias became High Priest. His name was Simon. And the High Priest was also the ruler of the country. So, during the time of the Maccabees, the Jews had a government in which the high priest was also the king. There is a big word for such a government. It is called a theocracy.

Nowadays, we believe in separating the government from religion, because in each country there may be people of several different religions, and it would not be fair to have one rule over the other. So in this broader way we follow the idea of religious freedom, the original idea the Maccabees fought for.

Sometimes it takes hundreds of years for an idea to become full grown.

The first Maccabees saved Jewish worship for us. If it had not been for them, there might be no synagogue today. Their descendants ruled in Jerusalem for many years. During this time, Jewish ideas had a chance to grow. And you will see how the Jews of that time thought of some wonderful ideas which the whole world uses today.

One of their most important ideas was that all children should go to school. The school became a part of the synagogue. Thus, learning and worship had the same home. The synagogue began to be a house of study as well as a house of worship.

THINKING ABOUT WHAT YOU HAVE LEARNED

1. Why is Alexander remembered as one conqueror of Palestine whom they liked so much they named their children after him?

2. Why has Hanukah become known "as the holiday of religious freedom"?

PARENTS

1. How can the idea of religious freedom be used in greeting cards which your family sends out for Hanukah?

2. Are there ways in which religious freedom is still not practiced in our country today?

Elephants used by the Syrian army

How the Synagogue became a house of study

CHAPTER XVI

The first Rabbis were teachers

You HAVE SEEN HOW the Maccabees saved the Temple as their most important house of worship. But the synagogues that had been started after the Jews lost their first Temple were not forgotten. Instead, when the king-priests of the Maccabees were at the head of our people, synagogues grew up all around the Temple.

The chief place of worship was the Temple. You know that Jews brought their gifts to the Temple, but they also worshipped in their "meeting places," closer to their homes. These synagogues grew in numbers, and they were not only outside but also inside the city of Jerusalem. We are told that in the last years of the rule of the Maccabees, there were 480 synagogues in Jerusalem alone.

On special occasions the Jews went to the great Temple to worship, but they also worshipped in their synagogues, day by day, and they studied in their synagogues. You have learned how the synagogue became a house of worship. Now you will see how the synagogue, which belongs to us, and also to the his-

tory of our people, became a house of study.

You will hear the stories of the first rabbis, and see how they were primarily teachers and how they made schools, so that every Jew could learn how to live as a Jew. Even the word "rabbi" is a word that means "teacher." And when we speak of Moses, we often call him "Moshe Rabbenu," which means "Moses our Teacher."

There is a story that our knowledge, which is the Torah, has been handed down in a living chain. Moses received the Torah on Mount Sinai and handed it to Joshua, and Joshua handed it down to the elders, who gave it in their turn to the prophets, and from the prophets it came to the men of the Great Assembly.

The Men of the Great Assembly

Who were the Men of the Great Assembly? They were scholars of the Torah who were assembled to discuss the laws. There were seventy of them, and you may think of them as the first congress to help the kings, but it was not exactly the same. It was more like what we call an academy of great scholars and thinkers. In later years it was called the Sanhedrin.

And this academy chose rabbis, who were entitled to teach the people and their children the Torah. Because the Sanhedrin was an academy of scholars, it could decide when a man was learned enough and pure enough to be a rabbi. And the Sanhedrin refused to send a rabbi to a synagogue unless the synagogue had a school.

The first rabbis

Now you see how closely the school and the synagogue were tied together. Let us see what it meant to be a rabbi in those days and whether the rabbis were like our rabbis of today.

You know that our rabbi of today is much more than a teacher. And his teaching is done in different ways. Sometimes he may not teach any classes in school. He teaches in his sermons, and he does many other things.

He performs the ceremonies for the most important events in our lives, at births, and at marriages, and at funerals. He leads us in the prayers for the Sabbath and the holidays. He supervises our schools. He may also teach some of the classes.

So our rabbi spends all of his time at his tasks. But in the beginning, in the old days, many of these tasks did not exist. The rabbi was more of a teacher and a scholar. The first rabbis spent only part of their time at this kind of synagogue work.

Our Torah handed down in a living chain

A rabbi could be a woodcutter, or a shoemaker, or a baker, or a blacksmith, or a scribe. He would pass half or two-thirds of the day working at his trade and earning a living. And the rest of his time would be spent in studying the Torah. He would read the scrolls over and over again, so that he knew some of them by heart. Then he would discuss them with other scholars, and give his ideas about questions that had more than one answer.

People might come to him with questions about how to observe the Sabbath, or how to treat a slave. He would think of all the laws on this subject, and if none of them seemed quite to apply, he would put two passages together, or find a story that might apply.

Daily worship

For instance, far back when the Jews in Babylon began to gather together to pray and to form a kind of synagogue, somebody might ask how many times a day worship should be held.

One scribe might remind them that sacrifices in the Temple were offered twice daily. But other scholars would say that everyone should worship three times a day because different verses in the Bible tell how Abraham prayed in the morning, and Isaac in the afternoon, and Jacob at night. So you see, if they knew the Bible well, they could put the rules together from different parts of the Bible.

Some rabbis also found a verse in the Psalms which speaks of prayer "evening, morning, and noon." And they read in the Book of Daniel how Daniel prayed three times a day. And so they could say, "You see, the Bible tells us to pray three times daily."

Soon certain teachers became famous for their wisdom, and people came from far away to sit at their feet. In those days, the students really sat on the ground before the teacher who explained the Torah.

When many students came to one teacher, he had to spend more time away from his trade. All by itself, a school had formed around him. These early rabbis did not want to accept money for their teaching of the Torah. They believed that no man should make of the Torah "a spade with which to dig." But in order to live, if they gave so much time to their teaching, they had to accept money for the hours they would otherwise have spent at their trade.

Thus, the first schools for teaching and explaining the Torah probably grew up in Babylonia during the time of exile. We do not have exact records about this, but we think that first there must have been schools to teach scribes how to copy the Torah and to answer questions about parts that were not clear.

When many Jews returned from Babylonia to Palestine, they kept on with the idea of teaching the Torah. Even though the priests again could make sacrifices, the new idea of the synagogue and of teaching the Torah was continued.

Now you may wonder, what was the difference between the Temple and the synagogue, between the priests and the rabbis. The Temple was the place for ceremonies and sacrifices. Its priests were members of a special family.

The synagogues were meeting places for discussion and teaching. And the rabbis did not have to be members of special families.

And you will see that when the Temple and the priesthood ended, the synagogue and the rabbis carried on. One of the reasons was that the most intelligent of the people could become rabbis even if they had no money to pay for their studies. For at this time, two thousand years ago, the Jews were the first to start free schools.

A school during the days of the Talmud

Schools for rich and poor alike

The first schools that we know about were not like our grammar schools. They were advanced schools. And to spend time with an advanced teacher required money. Then people began to say that the best and smartest boys were not always the sons of rich people. A shepherd might have a son who had the talent to be a rabbi. And they said it would be a pity for the brain of the shepherd's son to be wasted, or even slowed up for many years, because he had no money to study.

So the Sanhedrin thought about this question. And it decided that free high schools should be started for all boys of sixteen who wanted to get ready for college.

When they decided to start these schools, the question was asked, where shall the classes be held? And everyone said, "Why, in the synagogue," because by then there were synagogues in every town, and many in Jerusalem. So you see, we are still doing the same thing, having classes in the synagogue.

After a time people said that very bright boys who came to high school from ignorant homes ought to have a chance to start their studies when they were younger. Besides, more and more people wanted their children to learn to read and to learn to discuss the laws. So then it was decided that there should be elementary schools in every town and city. And that boys should start to school at the age of six. Just as we do today.

All parents were urged to send their boys to these elementary classes, which were also held in the synagogue building. In fact, as we have said, no rabbi was allowed to live in a town which did not provide classes for its children.

The Sanhedrin

Who did not allow it? The King? The Priests? No. This rule was made by the Sanhedrin, which supervised the rabbis. It could even decide when a 97

The Sanhedrin

student was ready to be a rabbi. It was Ezra the Scribe who started the Sanhedrin in Jerusalem, when the Jews came back from Babylon. You remember how Ezra found everything in confusion, and the Jews scattered in many parts of Palestine. He thought it would be a good thing to bring together the wisest men from every part of the country, to help him decide on questions of the Law. For Ezra did not want to be a dictator about deciding what the Torah meant, when ways of life had changed and the meaning was not clear. He remembered what Moses had done. He remembered the seventy Elders that Moses had assembled. So while the Second Temple was being built, seventy wise men were chosen, and these men met in Jerusalem, and came to be known as the Men of the Great Assembly.

But as you know, Palestine was still governed for many years by the Babylonians and the Syrians and the Greeks. So the Men of the Great Assembly did not have much power. And gradually we cease to hear about them.

But when the Maccabees drove the foreign rulers out, and the Jews could govern themselves, they called the Assembly together again. This time it was known as the Sanhedrin.

The seventy rabbis of the Sanhedrin had a special hall in the Temple grounds. They sat in a circle. In the center was the president, known as the Nasi, or ruler. At the right hand of the Nasi was the Ab Beth Din. Ab means father, Beth means house, and Din means law. He was the Elder, or father, of the House of Law.

Then there sat three rows of scholars, who were ready to fill the place of any members of the Sanhedrin who were absent.

The discussions in the Sanhedrin were about the meaning of the Law. For example, suppose you were in the Sanhedrin and a question arose about the fruit of a tree that grew near a fence. Suppose one man claimed the apples on his side of the fence belonged to him, and the other man claimed they were his apples because the tree grew on his side. Suppose the first man proved that the roots of the tree reached under the fence into his land. Then who owned the apples?

98

First, the rabbis of the Sanhedrin would try to remember whether such a question had already been decided, just as our lawyers today try to find a case like their own and show how it was decided. One rabbi might find a law that applied to branches that reached over a fence. Then another rabbi might say, but that law tells us nothing about the roots. Then a third rabbi might recite a passage from the Bible about roots. Then still another rabbi might tell a fable or an amusing story about roots. Such a story is called a parable. In Hebrew it is called a midrash. He might make up a midrash about two farmers who dug up their land, following the twisting roots from one side of the fence to the other, until the tree fell down and died and was of no use to either of them.

When the discussion in the Sanhedrin was finished, a vote would be taken. And thus, new laws were made.

The living chain of knowledge

Now, there was one important difference between the Sanhedrin and our Congress of the United States. Any citizen can run for Congress. But members of the Sanhedrin had to be rabbis. To become a rabbi, a student did not receive a diploma. When he finished his studies with his teacher, he received a special kind of blessing, which was called the Semiha.

We do not know exactly who performed the Semiha, but it was probably one of the chief Elders of the Sanhedrin who put his hands on the head of the student and pronounced the blessing that made him a rabbi. Thus he became a servant of God's laws. And he would then also be eligible for the Sanhedrin.

In our day, the rabbi takes care of our religious needs. We do not have a Sanhedrin, or a religious government. But the custom of the Semiha has been kept; in many rabbinical colleges, when a student finishes his work he is given the Semiha by the head of the college. With this blessing he becomes a rabbi.

And so you see that from the beginning until today, our rabbis have been students of the Torah, who brought the Torah to the people. The living chain of knowledge of the Torah that was handed from Moses to Joshua, and from Joshua to the Elders, is brought to the people by the rabbis, in the synagogues. And it is brought to the children in the synagogue schools.

THINKING ABOUT WHAT YOU HAVE LEARNED

1. How does the work of your Rabbi differ from the work of the early Rabbis?
2. How did the early Rabbis become lawmakers as well as teachers?

PARENTS

1. How does your family show that learning is considered very important?
2. A Rabbi helps to teach by answering questions. What question would your parents have asked the Rabbi if they had been visiting your class when he came?

CHAPTER XVII

How a poor boy became a great Rabbi

SUPPOSE THERE WERE NO schools. How would you answer all the questions that come into your head? If you have a little brother or sister, you know how they are always asking questions. Why, why, why? And only a few years ago, you yourself began to ask questions. Your father and mother were patient and tried to answer all your questions, but sometimes they laughed and said they only wished you would start to go to school. Because mothers and fathers have work to do, they can't spend all their time teaching their children. Instead, in a school, one teacher takes care of a whole group of children. The children get an equal chance to learn, and a teacher can be more expert than a parent.

This seems a very natural idea to you, but it was not always so. In the ancient days, children learned only from their mothers and fathers. Two thousand years ago, that was true in all countries. In a few countries, even today, there are just beginning to be schools for everybody. We call them backward countries. But in Judea, two thousand years ago, the Jews started a system of schools for all boys starting at the age of six.

You know that every synagogue had to have a school where all boys could learn to read, and could begin to study the Torah. But what did they do if they wanted to go on to higher studies? Just as today, they would try to go to college. But in those days the colleges were not like ours of today, great universities with hundreds of teachers. In those days a college would be started around a wise scholar, whose fame spread until more and more pupils came from far and wide to study with him. Usually the college would be named after the teacher.

You have already seen that the teachers of those days did not believe in taking money for teaching the Torah. The custom was for a man to earn his living at a regular trade, and not to take money for teaching God's word. But there are other expenses to running a school, and as more students came to the colleges, these expenses grew. So the schools had doorkeepers, who took a small fee from the students for each lesson.

Some students were so poor that even this was a hardship. A student who did not come from a rich family had to earn his own way while he was going to school. He had to work his way through college.

A poor boy wins an education

In modern times, we also have stories about great men who wanted very badly to go to school, and who worked very hard to get their education. We have all heard stories about people working their way through college, like our stories about Abraham Lincoln, who walked so far to go to school. But the oldest of these stories goes way back to the old days in Babylon and Jerusalem, and it is about one of the greatest rabbis who ever lived. His name was Hillel. And he was the first student in all the world, whom we know about, to win a free scholarship.

Even today, when people talk about how poor they are, it is a custom to ask, "Are you as poor as Hillel?" And when we talk about someone's great wisdom, we ask, "Is he as wise as Hillel?" Let us see why his name is remembered in both these ways.

Hillel was born in Babylon, in the time when many Jews had returned to Jerusalem. But, as you know, a great many families remained in Babylonia.

Though he came from a poor family, Hillel was soon known as a bright scholar, and he managed to attend one of the best academies in Babylon. But

he heard of the great school of Shemaiah and Abtalion in Jerusalem and decided to go there, just as today students will travel all over the world to famous professors. Art students go to Paris, and medical students come from all parts of the world to Johns Hopkins University; lawyers go to Yale, students of English literature go to London, and students of Hebrew and Arabic go to Jerusalem.

So, two thousand years ago, there were already rivalries between famous Torah academies. Some said the best were in Babylonia, others said the newer schools that had grown up in Jerusalem were the best, since the Temple had been rebuilt, and the Sanhedrin was there.

So Hillel made his way to Jerusalem. He earned his living as a woodcutter, just as some college students today earn their living tending furnaces. Hillel used half of what he earned to live on and the other half to pay the doorkeeper so that he could go to his classes.

Hillel earns his living as a wood-cutter

One week Hillel had earned very little, and on Friday he did not have enough money to pay for his ticket to the classroom. He was very unhappy, as he did not want to miss a single lecture. So Hillel climbed upon the high window, and listened.

It happened to be a very cold day for Jerusalem, and Hillel listened so hard he did not notice he was freezing. He lost consciousness.

At dawn on Sabbath when the rabbi came to say his prayers, he found that the room was dark. Rabbi Shemaiah looked up and saw the form of a man through the window. He rushed out, with some of his students, and there they found Hillel, cold and unconscious.

The day was a Sabbath, but even so the rabbi hastily lighted a fire and heated water in which to bathe Hillel and revive him. For you know that when it is a question of saving a life, rules may be broken. And the rabbi said Hillel would live to keep many Sabbaths, and to teach many others to keep the Sabbath, and so it was a good deed.

When Rabbis Shemaiah and Abtalion learned what Hillel had gone through because he did not have enough money to get into the school, they said he should be admitted free. And that was the first scholarship that we know about.

The scholarship was certainly worthwhile, because some years later Hillel became the head of the same school and president of the Sanhedrin. And Hillel gave out many scholarships. He said that any student who could master the work should be allowed to attend the college, whether or not he could pay.

Two schools of thought

Hillel had a rival who was head of another college; his name was Shammai. And they stood for different ideas. Hillel had been poor and believed that even poor people should be allowed to study. Shammai's students were more apt to be from wealthy or priestly families.

They often disagreed about how the Law should be understood. Sometimes this was even a question of how the prayers should be recited. Shammai believed in the letter of the Law. For instance, he said the people should recite the most important prayer, the Shema ("Hear, O Israel, The Lord Our God, the Lord is One") in a certain way. He said they should do it while lying down, at night, and while they were standing up, in the morning, because the Bible says, "When thou liest down and when thou risest up." But Hillel believed in the spirit more than in the letter of the Law, and he said the prayer could be recited in any position, so long as it was recited in earnest. He reminded Shammai that the same Bible verse also said to recite the prayer "When thou walkest by the way." He said a man could recite a true prayer sitting, standing, lying down, or even while he was working in the field.

Shammai was also very strict about serving warm food on the Sabbath. He reminded people that lighting fires was forbidden, since it was work to light a fire. But Hillel said Sabbath was a day for rejoicing, and that people would find the day more enjoyable if they had a warm meal. So he said why not keep the

"Teach me the Torah while standing on one foot"

food warm in an oven that had already been lit on Friday? And that was what people did, and what some people still do.

And do you remember the "Hillel sandwich" which we eat on Passover? We place bitter herbs on a piece of matzo and eat it as a sandwich. Hillel started this custom.

The golden rule

And of course you must know the most important story about Hillel, because it is the story of the Golden Rule, by which the whole world tries to live— the rule that is the same for Christians and Jews, and indeed for all religions.

The story is about an impatient man who came to Shammai and said he did not have time to learn the whole Torah. He wanted Shammai to teach him only the most important parts. Shammai chased him away. The same man came to Hillel, and said he wanted to learn as much of the Torah as he could learn while standing on one foot.

Now Hillel was known as a man of very great patience, a man who never

became angry. So he treated this man with patience and wisdom. For Hillel would never chase away anyone who wanted to learn, even if he wanted to learn in an impossible way. So he answered the mocker, who wanted to learn while standing on one foot.

"Do not do unto others as you would not have them do unto you," said Rabbi Hillel. "That is the whole Torah. All the rest is commentary." And he added, "Now go and study."

The wise sayings of Hillel

We see in this story why Hillel was one of the greatest of all teachers. For he did not turn away an impossible 103 question. He found an answer that has rung through the ages. And with the answer he also made the pupil feel the need to study the great knowledge that was contained within the answer.

There are many other wise sayings of Hillel, and stories about Hillel, that have come down to us. One of his wise sayings is, "Separate not thyself from thy community." This means that a person should not think only of himself, in what he does, but should think of the whole community. It means that a rich man or a scholar should not separate himself from those who have less or know less than he does. It also means that there is love between a man and his fellowmen, that there is help for him in his community when he needs it.

It means that in our own Jewish community we find the wisdom and the warmth of our whole past. The synagogue has always been the center of the Jewish community, the place where people met, where they studied, where they worshipped. So Hillel's warning was that it is bad for a person to be selfish and alone.

But he did not teach people to be exactly like everyone else, just because they were part of the community. A great saying of Hillel's has come down to us as a riddle, and as a song. It goes:

"If I'm not for myself,
Who will be for me?
But if I'm only for myself,
What am I?
And if not now, then when?"

You can write pages and pages about the great meaning of this saying, that tells us how to work for a balance in our lives. It tells us to believe in ourselves, but not to be selfish. It tells us to make use of every moment of our lives.

Hillel believed that people should keep on learning all their lives, not for gain but for the sake of learning itself, for the sake of a better understanding of men and of God. "He who adds not to his learning, diminishes it," Hillel said.

The letter of the law

We have another story about Hillel's teaching, which shows us the deep difference between the two ways of thinking about the Torah. As you have seen, one group believed in the literal meaning of the Law, following it just as it was written down, and the other group believed that the Law had to be explained so that it would apply to all of human ways, so that it would not be too strict for people.

At this time there were two parties about a hundred years old. One party had more wealthy persons and important members of the priestly families. They were called the Sadducees; they believed in the strict letter of the law as written in the Bible, and they were the most important people in Temple worship, in ceremonies and rituals.

The other groups were the Pharisees, many of whom came from the ordinary people. They believed not only in the letter of the Torah, but also in the explanations of the great rabbis, in the sayings called the "oral" or spoken law.

We might say that the priests were more important in the first party, and the rabbis or teachers were more important in the second party. There were men of both parties in the Sanhedrin. And Hillel tried to find ways of making peace between them. But we feel from his teachings that he was at heart with the more democratic people, the Pharisees.

An example of how Hillel believed in the human sayings, as well as in the strict letter of the law, is in a story of how a man came to Hillel and asked what was the Jewish Law. Hillel answered that it was partly written down, and that part of it had been handed down by word of mouth. The man said he believed in the first part, but not in the second part. He wanted to study the written Law, but as he could not read, he wanted Hillel first to teach him the alphabet.

Hillel, with his usual patience, agreed, and he began to teach the man his aleph

Hillel explaining the written and the oral law

beth, or his a, b, c's. But on the second day he taught the man differently. When Hillel wrote down "a," he made the sound of "z" and when he wrote down "b" he spoke the sound of "w," and so on, mixing everything up. His pupil said, "But yesterday you made different sounds for these letters! How can I tell the meaning of what you write? It all depends on how you explain it!"

"Exactly," said Hillel. And he showed that the written Law, too, had to be explained, because the life of a people could change. Rabbis and men of God were needed to explain the changes and the new things that happened in each generation.

So you see that Hillel taught that it was important for a man to understand how to live a good life, how to love his fellowmen. Just as important as observing all the rules of ritual. And you will see how, when the Temple was destroyed a second time, and when the priests disappeared, it was the rabbis, the teachers, who saved Judaism. For as had been proven before in Babylonia, the armies of the enemy could destroy the Temple, but they could not destroy the word of God, they could not destroy what Moses and Ezra and Hillel and other great rabbis taught.

THINKING ABOUT WHAT YOU HAVE LEARNED

1. What made Hillel's teachers decide to give him a scholarship so he wouldn't have to pay to get into school?
2. How did Hillel explain the "Oral Law" by his way of teaching the alphabet?

PARENTS

1. Ask your parents if they know any stories about people who had to work hard to get their education.
2. Do they remember the "why" questions which you asked when you were young?

CHAPTER XVIII

How a School saved Judaism

YOU KNOW THE REASON why Jews are still together today, still a people, when all the other peoples of those early times are gone. It is because our synagogues, which were houses of study as well as houses of worship, kept us together. Suppose there had been no schools, suppose only a few priests had known how to read and how to keep our Law. Then when an enemy captured Judea, all he would have had to do would have been to arrest all the priests, or kill them. Then the enemy would teach all the Jewish children his own laws and his own way of worship, and they would stop being Jews.

You remember how this nearly happened when the Jews were conquered by the Babylonians, and lost the First Temple. But we saw how Jewish worship was saved when Ezra and the scribes wrote down the laws, and taught them to the people.

And you remember that Jewish worship was nearly destroyed again when the Greek and Syrian generals conquered the Jews. But it was saved by

the Maccabees, who drove out the enemy. And during the reign of the Maccabees, the rabbis started schools for all boys, so the Law should never be forgotten. You will see how the study of the Torah kept the Jews together.

Judea reconquered

During the time of Rabbi Hillel, trouble started again in Judea. And soon after his death, there was warfare, and Israel was invaded again. This time the enemy came from across the sea, from a land that is now called Italy. But in those days long ago the people of Italy were called Romans. In fact, the capital of Italy is still named after them, because it is called Rome.

So it was the turn of the Romans to try to rule the world.

If you look at the map, you will notice that the countries we are talking about make a circle around the Mediterranean Sea. If you start with Egypt, you can go around the rim of the sea to Israel, and Syria, and Greece, and Italy. And the strange thing is that in the old days each

ITALY

Rome

Black Sea

GREECE

SYRIA

Mediterranean Sea

PALESTINE

●Jerusalem

NORTH AFRICA

EGYPT

of these countries took a turn in becoming strong and in trying to conquer all the other countries. That is, each of the countries except Judea; the Jews only wanted to be left alone in peace. But they were never left alone for very long.

You remember that the Egyptians marched through the Jewish country, to conquer Syria. Then the Syrians marched back, to conquer Egypt. Then the Greeks and Syrians see-sawed back

108

to conquer Egypt. And now it was the turn of the Romans. They conquered their way around the sea. They conquered Palestine too, and they ruled over the Jews as the Syrians had done. At first they did not trouble the Jews in their worship. So the Jews said, let them rule, "so long as we can worship God in our synagogues and our Temple."

Then there came a Roman emperor named Caligula. He wanted the Jews to worship him instead of God. He wanted his own statue put up in the Temple! He was even worse than the Syrian king Antiochus, who wanted Greek gods to be put up in the Temple. You remember how the Maccabees revolted against the mad king Antiochus. And so, two hundred years later, Jews began to fight against the Emperor Caligula. Secret bands raided Roman camps. In the end, a big Roman army came to capture Jerusalem. And it was a terrible war, because the Jews had to fight hard and long for their holy city and their Temple.

The Romans surrounded Jerusalem and tried to starve out the Jews. The Jewish fighters closed all the gates to the city, and no one could get in or out. For weeks the siege went on. But it was not an even fight. The Romans had more soldiers, and more weapons, and more chariots than the Jews. They had the strongest army in the world. And some of the wise men in Jerusalem saw that it was only a matter of time before the city would fall. And they said, "The most important thing is to save the Law." They remembered the other times that Jerusalem had fallen, and the Temple had been destroyed, but that even so the people had gone on, because the Law was saved.

The greatest of Hillel's pupils

One of these wise men was Rabbi Johanan ben Zaccai. He was a great teacher; as a boy he had sat at the feet of Rabbi Hillel. And he was the next in the chain of great teachers of the Torah.

He must have been a wonderful pupil, because the stories about him tell us that he was always the first to come to the house of study, and that he was always the last to leave. From his teacher, Hillel, he learned never to be boastful, even of learning. And Rabbi Johanan ben Zaccai said, "If you have learned a great deal of the Torah, do not take credit for it, because learning the Torah was the purpose for which you were created."

He was very modest about his own knowledge as compared to that of his teacher, the great Hillel. He said that if all the sky became parchment, and all the trees were pens, and all the seas became ink, and all men became scribes, it would not be enough to record the knowledge that was his teacher's. But even with all the help that Hillel had given him, ben Zaccai said that he had only taken from the wisdom of Hillel as much as a fly might take in drinking from the ocean. Yet his modest idea of himself was not shared by his teacher, for although Johanan ben Zaccai was the youngest pupil of the aged Hillel, the teacher had already prophesied that Johanan ben Zaccai would be the greatest of his pupils. Hillel called him "the father of wisdom" and the "father of the coming generations." And this proved true, because when Jerusalem was about to fall, Rabbi Johanan ben Zaccai gave all his thoughts to saving the academy and the teaching of the Torah, and by saving the school he saved the synagogue, and he saved the future of Judaism.

How the Romans were fooled

How did Rabbi Johanan ben Zaccai manage to save the Law? He gathered together a few of his most devoted students, and he told them of his secret plan. First, they were to spread the story that he was very sick. This would not be difficult, for disease and starvation were spreading in the besieged city. Then the students were to say that the rabbi had died. They were to put him in a coffin, and carry him to the city gate. They were to tell the commander that they had to carry him out to bury him, since the cemetery was outside the city walls.

Permission was granted. But once Rabbi Johanan ben Zaccai was outside the walls of Jerusalem, he made his way to the Roman army camp, and asked to see the commander, General Vespasian. The Roman soldiers did not think that the aged Jewish scholar could be dangerous. Perhaps they thought he even bore a message of surrender. They took him to the General. ''Hail, Emperor Vespasian!'' said the rabbi.

The General was surprised. The fact was that he hoped he would some day become the Emperor of Rome. As Rabbi Johanan ben Zaccai was a wise man, he must have heard this story about the General and he must have thought it would be helpful to flatter the General in order to get what he wanted. But the strange thing is that on that very same day a messenger arrived from Rome with the news that General Vespasian had been made emperor!

So the General felt sure that the wise old rabbi was a prophet. And he was ready to give him what he wanted.

The rabbi asked for a small thing. He asked to be allowed to continue teaching the Torah, in a town called Yabneh, near the sea.

The Emperor-General was surprised. It seemed so small a wish. But if that was all the strange old Jew wanted, he

Johanan ben Zaccai arising from his coffin

was glad to let him have his wish. And Johanan ben Zaccai departed from the Roman camp to found the Academy of Yabneh.

Jewish learning is saved

It was this academy that saved the Torah. For the Romans captured Jerusalem. And the Romans destroyed the Second Temple, just as the Babylonians had destroyed the First Temple. But because there was a college of the Torah in the small town of Yabneh, Jewish learning was not destroyed. The soldiers could not destroy what was in the heads and hearts of the Jews. That is why we say the pen is stronger than the sword.

Students came to Rabbi Johanan ben Zaccai in Yabneh. And while the Sanhedrin, the Jewish court of law, was ended in Jerusalem, a new court, with the same number of rabbis, was established in Yabneh.

The priestly sacrifices of the Temple were ended, but the study of the Law continued. The school was called the "vineyard of Yabneh" because the sages there gathered the words of the Law that were as grapes on the vine, and from the grapes they pressed the wine of wisdom.

Years later, when Rabbi Johanan visited the ruins of Jerusalem, and found a rabbi sitting and weeping in the ruins of the Temple, he reminded him of a saying of the Prophet Hosea. "The knowledge of God is more desirable than burnt offerings." And it was the knowledge of God that had been saved, for in Yabneh the Jews could keep on with their studies and their worship in the synagogue.

Even while the Romans ruled Palestine, the Jews quietly took their problems to the academy in Yabneh. Once more they paid taxes to a foreign ruler, but they followed their own beliefs. There were very bad years ahead for the Jews, but through the years Jewish laws were saved by the human chain of rabbis and teachers, who kept the synagogue alive.

THINKING ABOUT WHAT YOU HAVE LEARNED

1. Why did the Roman general Vespasian offer Johanan ben Zaccai a reward?
2. How did Johanan comfort the Rabbi whom he saw weeping over the ruins of the second Temple?

PARENTS

1. Ask your parents to tell you some ways in which the Romans are remembered in world history.
2. What do your parents think would have happened to Judaism if the Temple had not been destroyed by the Romans?

CHAPTER XIX

How Rabbi Akiba gave his life for the Torah

Now some very bad years arrived for the Jews. After the Romans captured Jerusalem and destroyed the Temple, the whole country was poor. Just as in times long before, when the Babylonians had driven the Jews into captivity, the Romans now dragged away many of the Jews, and sold them as slaves.

Years of recovery

But in the villages and on the farms life went on. People lived quietly and tended their flocks. They came together in their small synagogues, and they kept the laws of the Torah. And in the quiet village of Yabneh, the best rabbis and students kept on with their studies.

They did not try to do very much. They just tried to keep Judaism alive. For the Jewish people were like a man who has been terribly and brutally beaten. It takes him some time to gain back his strength.

After ten or twenty years, those who had been children during the terrible war grew up. And those who had been young men were men in their prime.

They raised their heads again. They wanted to do something with their lives. But they had to be very careful because the Romans were terribly strong.

As always, the Jews decided to be stronger in their minds, to study and to try to know God.

The story of Rabbi Akiba

One such Jew was named Akiba. He had been only a lad of seventeen when the Temple was destroyed. And though he was a bright lad, in the bad times that came afterward he had not done anything with his mind. It seemed that the best a man could do in those difficult times was to live a quiet life. So Akiba was a shepherd.

Yet even in his own little village, people felt he was someone with special gifts. Very often, a woman will notice this in a man, even while he is poor and unknown, and she will try to help him to bring out the best that is in himself. And so we have a wonderful love story that has come down to us, about Akiba and Rachel.

Rachel was the most beautiful girl in the town, and she was the daughter of the richest Jew in the town. For even in those bad times, there were men who had begun to recover their wealth.

Rachel fell in love with the bright young shepherd, Akiba. When her father heard that she wanted to marry the poor, ignorant shepherd, he thought the shepherd was after her money. And so he said he would give her nothing. He would disinherit her.

But Akiba and Rachel said they did not want her father's wealth. After they were married, Akiba told his wife that he was ashamed of being only an ignorant shepherd.

His wife said, "Why don't you go and study?"

"But I am too old," he said. "I am a grown, married man."

She reminded him that even the aged rabbis kept on studying. There was Johanan ben Zaccai, who had stolen his way out of Jerusalem to keep on studying the Torah. "If the aged rabbis are not too old to learn," she said, "why are you too old? And the longer you wait, the harder it will be."

Akiba thought about this. He recalled the saying of the great Rabbi Hillel, the saying that everybody knew. "If not now, then when?"

But there was another difficulty. If he wanted to study, he would have to leave his village, and go to an academy at Lydda. And he would not be able to support his wife. He would not even be able to support himself while he studied.

Rachel said he was not to worry about her. She would take care of herself, and she would wait for him until he finished college.

"But it may take twelve years," Akiba said.

"Then I will wait twelve years."

And Akiba went away. The story is told that when he went away, he had a parting gift from his wife. She had cut her beautiful hair and sold it, so that Akiba would have some money to start him on his studies.

For twelve years Akiba remained at

Akiba hears his wife talking

the academy. He was known as the hardest working of all the students. At the end of twelve years, he came home to his village. And there is another very touching part of the story about Akiba and his wife. As he approached their hut, it is told, he heard his wife talking to a neighbor.

"Your husband has stayed away for twelve years," the neighboring woman was saying. "Don't you think it is time he took care of you?"

"He is studying," Rachel said. "And if he wants to study for another twelve years, I shall not complain."

Then, without even seeing his wife, although he longed for her very much, Akiba turned back. He studied another twelve years, and when he returned home, he was the most famous rabbi in all the academy. He was followed, we are told, by a parade of thousands of students who wished to do him honor, and to honor his wife, Rachel.

The task of Rabbi Akiba

Rabbi Akiba became head of a college. And he worked on a task that had been worked upon by Rabbi Hillel, and by Johanan ben Zaccai. This task was to put the Torah laws in order.

You remember that the first time the Temple was destroyed, and the Jews were taken to Babylon, there arose a scribe named Ezra who said that the Torah should be copied down, and studied. So in that way, the destruction of the Temple made the Law even stronger.

Now, the second time the Temple was destroyed, there arose Rabbi Akiba, who said that the laws must be arranged in order, so they would be easier to keep and to follow. For there were hundreds of scrolls, and there were the sayings of many wise rabbis who had explained the laws. To arrange the Torah, and to arrange the sayings of the rabbis, would again make the Law stronger.

Some scrolls were known to have contained the words of Moses, and of the great prophets like Jeremiah and Isaiah, who heard the word of God. And there were also other scrolls and stories that were not as important. For many years rabbis had been deciding which scrolls should be kept together as the "true" Torah. And now in the time of Akiba, this work was being finished.

Our scholars of today believe that the books of the Bible were finally put together by Rabbi Akiba and the Sanhedrin of his time. And while they were deciding what should go into the Bible itself, they were arranging all the explanations of the law into a very big book that is called the Mishnah.

This task went on from one generation of rabbis to another, and it was several lifetimes before it was done. But a great part of it was done by Rabbi Akiba. And so important did it become that even the Romans became worried.

Under penalty of death

They said "The Jews are still following their own laws instead of our laws. More and more of them are studying their laws." And the Romans decided to put a stop to it, for they knew that as long as the Jews kept their laws, they would one day try to revolt and gain

The fable of the fox and the fish

their independence again.

So the Romans forbade the Jews to teach the Torah to their children. They closed all the schools in all the towns. But Akiba would not give up. He gathered his best students around him, and found a secret place, a cave, in which they could study. The students had to take turns as lookouts because the penalty for teaching the Torah was death.

Many Jews had given up resisting the Romans. They had taken up Roman ways, just as hundreds of years before Jews had taken up the ways of the Greeks. And there was such a Jew, named Pappus, who knew Akiba, and who asked him why he was risking his life to teach the Torah. Akiba answered by telling him a story, for you know that a story with a moral is often the best way to answer a question. Akiba's fable was about the fox and the fish.

The fox came alongside the stream and talked to the fish. "I came here to give you a warning," he said. "Some fishermen are coming, so beware! Why don't you come out of the water, and they will never catch you!"

"You're not so wise as you are supposed to be, O fox," said the fish. "If I come out of the water, I will die right away. But if I stay in the water, I can at least try not to get caught by the fisherman."

"So you see," Rabbi Akiba explained to Pappus, "A Jew without the Torah is like a fish out of water. He will surely die. But with the Torah he is at home, like a fish in water. As long as a Jew stays with his Torah, he will be alive, and he can at least try to escape his enemies."

Akiba blesses Bar Kochba

A star of Judah

And there was another thing Akiba said about the fish. Even if caught, he can put up a fight. So when the Roman soldiers came after the Jews who were still teaching the Torah, a revolt began, just as in the days of the Maccabees. This time the name of the leader was Bar Kochba. This means the Son of the Star. And there was a prophecy that a Star of Judah would arise, to save the Jews in time of trouble. Rabbi Akiba believed the prophecy and he believed the time had come, because the troubles of the Jews were so great that the star had surely arisen.

He was a very old man by then. But he had the courage of a young man, and he joined the revolt. He gave his blessing to Bar Kochba.

The Romans were very strong, stronger than the Greeks had been. And Bar Kochba was not as successful against the Romans as the Maccabees had been against the Greeks. The men of Bar Kochba fought valiantly, from hills and caves. The vowed they would rather all die than live in other ways than Jewish ways, without the Torah. And the fighters were slain, almost to the last man.

Rabbi Akiba was caught by the Romans, and even though he was very old and a famous scholar, he was put to death. With his last breath, he uttered the Shema Yisrael, "Hear, O Israel, the Lord our God, the Lord is One."

The lesson of Akiba

But even with the death of Bar Kochba and his men, even with the death of Rabbi Akiba, the Romans did not conquer the Torah. For other Rabbis continued to study and to teach. They remembered a lesson of Rabbi Akiba when he had been asked which was more important, the study of the Law or the practice of the Law. Some Rabbis said the practice was more important, but Rabbi Akiba said, "Study is greater, for study brings practice."

The Rabbis also said, "Rabbi Akiba will be a warning to the poor who do not study. When they are asked why they have not studied the Law, and they answer, because they were poor and had to work for a living, then Rabbi Akiba will be held up as one of those who was very poor and yet studied." They also remembered a saying of Rabbi Akiba, "Study the Law in thy old age, even if thou hast not studied it in thy youth. Do not say, I do not need to study because I am old, but study it always." He did this in his own life, and he helped to put together the Torah that keeps us together.

THINKING ABOUT WHAT YOU HAVE LEARNED

1. Why did the Romans try to prevent the Jews from studying the Torah?
2. What was Akiba's answer to the question: "Which is greater—study or practice?"

PARENTS

1. Do your parents know of any stories like that of Akiba in which people began to study after they were grown up?
2. Do your parents know of any stories in which a wife made many sacrifices to help her husband study for a career?

A coin of Akiba's time

CHAPTER XX

How a Rabbi told stories
to teach the Torah

WE HAVE BEEN LEARNING about the great troubles that came upon the Jewish people, and how, through all their troubles, they clung to the Law. Even in the old days, when the Jews had seen their Temple destroyed once by the Babylonians, and another time by the Romans, it was said, "If any other people had gone through what Israel has gone through, they would have given up the Law."

The living chain unbroken

And a great rabbi said, "That is exactly why God gave the Torah to the Jews. He knew they were a very stubborn people. They were called a stiff-necked people because they were so stubborn. And God knew they would never give up the Torah no matter what happened to them." This was the next great rabbi in our chain, and his name was Rabbi Meir. His name means "To Shed Light."

Just as Rabbi Akiba, when he was a young man, had lived through the war when the Romans destroyed the Second Temple, so Rabbi Meir was a young man during the last stand of Bar Kochba. And he was one of those who carried on the study of the Torah after Rabbi Akiba had been killed by the Romans.

Once more the Romans carted off into slavery the best and strongest of the Jews, those who had not been killed in Bar Kochba's revolt. The cities and the farms were ruined. Jews who had not been captured as slaves fled to Egypt and to ancient Babylonia and to Greece. But in spite of all this, there were some who kept up the study of the Torah in Palestine. For that was the name the Romans had given to the land of Judea and Israel.

We are told how one teacher even gave up his life to save his students, so that the living chain of knowledge would not be broken. And one of the students who was saved was the same Rabbi Meir who had been a pupil of Rabbi Akiba.

During the time of Bar Kochba's revolt against the Romans, when teaching the Torah was forbidden, the students had to scatter. And Rabbi Meir had to leave Rabbi Akiba. But he found another group of secret students in the hills near Jerusalem. Their teacher was also a very old man, Rabbi Judah ben Baba. They had a hiding place in the hills, but Roman spies found out where it was. One day the lookout sounded the warning that the Romans were coming.

The aged Rabbi Judah ben Baba told Meir and the other students, "Run quickly! I will delay the Romans!"

"And what will become of you?" Meir and the other pupils asked.

But their Rabbi commanded them to go, for in their young minds the Torah would live. The Roman troops arrived and they killed the brave old Rabbi Judah ben Baba, throwing three hundred spears at him. His students had scattered in all directions over the hills, and Meir was among those who were not caught.

After some years, there was a new emperor in Rome, and he was less harsh

Judah ben Baba warns his students

against the Jews. He allowed them to teach again. Rabbi Meir came out of hiding and started a new academy in the town of Usha. He continued the work of his greatest teacher, Rabbi Akiba. This work was to write down and to arrange the explanations of the Law in the Mishnah.

Rabbi Meir was himself a scribe; he earned his living by copying out books of the Torah. Some of them he had copied so many times that he knew them by heart. Once, when he was traveling, he came to a town at the time of the celebration of Purim, and found that the Jews of that town did not have the Scroll of Esther. So he sat down just before the holiday and wrote out the entire scroll exactly, from memory, without missing a single word.

Rabbi Meir could also remember the debates of all the great rabbis; it was said that he could give a hundred arguments on each side of a question. The importance of seeing both sides of a question is that it helps people to understand each other. And this leads to peace. That is why Jewish scholars have always tried to understand both sides of an argument.

The stories of Rabbi Meir

Rabbi Meir was famous for another gift, a gift for explaining the Torah by stories and fables. Many of his stories have come down to us today.

The story-telling side of the Torah was his specialty. As you know, many of the rabbis liked to give their explanations of the Law by examples or little stories. Rabbi Meir's favorite stories

were about animals and, like his beloved teacher Akiba, one of the animals he liked best to tell tales about was the fox. A follower of Rabbi Meir counted three hundred fables that he told about the fox.

We know Rabbi Akiba's story about the fox who tried to get the fish to come up out of the water. Rabbi Meir liked to tell a story about a fox who saw some ripe fruit hanging on the trees behind a garden wall. The fox wanted to eat the fruit, but he couldn't jump over the wall. He ran all around the garden and finally he found a hole in the wall. But he was too fat to get through the hole. So he sat down there for three days, fasting, until he got thin enough to slip through the hole. Then he gorged himself on the fruit. But when he tried to get back out of the garden, he found that he was again too fat. So he had to fast for three more days until he got thin enough to get out the way he had come in.

Meir's fable of the fox and the fruit

"Oh garden!" cried the fox, after he was outside the wall once more, "what delicious fruit you have! But what good are you to me? For all my work, and all my fasting, and all my cleverness, I am just as thin as I was before."

Then the Rabbi would explain to his listeners that a greedy man will have no more than the fox did for his troubles. "Man comes naked into the garden of the world," Rabbi Meir said, "and naked he must go out of it. For all his toil and trouble to gather worldly goods, he can carry nothing with him."

Advice to the Romans

Even the Romans must have heard of the wisdom of Rabbi Meir, for one day the Roman Emperor sent a message to the Jews of Palestine. "Send us one of your great lamps," the message said At first the rabbis did not understand what was meant. But finally they thought, "It is Rabbi Meir who is meant, because he sheds light." And so Rabbi Meir was sent to Rome, where he explained many of the Jewish beliefs to the Romans, and as a result there was less persecution of the Jewish scholars by the Emperor at that time.

One of his sayings was, "Travelers should go in threes. A single traveler may be attacked, and two may quarrel, but if there is a third, they will always make their way in peace."

Some of his advice was not about the Law but about manners. And it is good advice today. Rabbi Meir said that you should not press a friend to join you at a meal when you know he will not accept the invitation. You should not

Meir explaining Judaism to the Romans

heap presents on a man when you know he does not wish to accept them. Do not aggravate your friend when he is in a temper. Do not come into his house at the moment of his downfall.

Rabbi Meir believed in charity so strongly that even to this day many Jews keep charity boxes in their homes with his name written on the box. Whenever they drop a coin into the box, it is in memory of the great and good Rabbi Meir.

121

Teaching the Torah to children

Most important of all

And he believed, too, that the most important thing in all the world was to teach the Torah to our children. It was Rabbi Meir who told the story that we already know, the story of how God decided to give the Ten Commandments to the Israelites if they would pledge that the Commandments would be kept eternally.

First the people said they would pledge by their ancestors. But God answered that their ancestors had passed away.

Then the people said they would swear by their prophets. But God answered that their prophets, too, would pass away.

At last the people offered their children as a pledge. They promised to teach the Ten Commandments to their children, and that their children would teach it in turn to their children, and that the Commandments would be observed forever, from children to children's children. Then God said the pledge was perfect. And He gave the tablets of the Law to Moses.

From generation to generation

And so every time the Jews were conquered, they were not destroyed, because the Law was taught from generation to generation.

The Babylonians who conquered the Jews ceased to exist as a people. And the Romans who conquered the Jews ceased to be a people. But the Jewish Law remained and grew, for it was a living Law. As each great rabbi learned the Law, he added to it his own ideas, to help it fit the life of his own time. And so, by the time of the great rabbis, like Hillel and Johanan ben Zaccai, like Akiba and Meir, there were many definitions that went with each law.

And Rabbi Akiba had done much in the great task of sorting out these definitions, so that it would be easier to find all the ifs and buts that went with each law. Instead of having to look for them in many scattered scrolls, a scholar would find the rules that went with each main subject gathered together. This was a great task to do, and Rabbi Akiba did not finish it before he was killed by the Romans.

Rabbi Meir and many other scholars carried on his work. They divided Jewish learning into two main parts. The Torah itself was the "written Law" because it contained all the laws set down by Moses after he received the Commandments. And all the explanations of the Law, all the rules under the laws of Moses, were called the "oral laws," because they were the laws that had been spoken out during discussions by the rabbis.

Now, the time had come when no man could remember all these explanations and all the stories of the rabbis. You have seen how the work of writing down the "oral laws," the work of Rabbi Akiba, was continued by Rabbi Meir. It was finished by the next rabbi in the great chain, Judah HaNasi.

THINKING ABOUT WHAT YOU HAVE LEARNED

1. How did Rabbi Meir earn his living and how did this occupation help him as a Rabbi?

2. For what kind of stories is Rabbi Meir most famous? Do you remember one of them?

PARENTS

1. Ask your parents what is the greatest feat of memory they ever saw.

2. Rabbi Meir taught some rules of good manners regarding behavior toward other people. What are some rules your family has about good behavior?

A charity box

CHAPTER XXI

How the Chain of Rabbis made the Mishnah

NOWADAYS WHEN WE THINK of a book being written, we think of one person who sits in a room and writes the book. We know that sometimes that person has helpers to find the facts for him. And we know that it can take many years for a person to write a very important book. Sometimes a man spends his whole life on a book.

But we have been reading about a Jewish book, the Mishnah, that took more than one lifetime to write. It was written by a living chain of rabbis, each of whom spent much of his lifetime in this work. Rabbi Hillel worked on gathering together our laws and explanations of the laws, and then Rabbi Johanan ben Zaccai, who was a pupil of Hillel, carried on the great work. And then Rabbi Akiba, who was a pupil of Johanan ben Zaccai, did his share. And then Rabbi Meir, the Shedder of Light, who was a pupil of Rabbi Akiba, carried on the writing of the Mishnah. But even he did not finish.

The rabbi of rabbis

The book was finished by the next rabbi in this living chain, whose name was Judah HaNasi. He was called "The Rabbi," because he was so famous.

So strongly did the Jews believe in the living chain of knowledge that there were some who said that when a great rabbi dies, another great rabbi is born on the same day. Perhaps this story arose from the fact that Judah HaNasi was indeed born on the same day that Rabbi Akiba was put to death by the Romans.

Of course it could not have been known on the day of his birth that he would become a great rabbi, although his family had such hopes for him, just as every family in all the ages hopes that each child will become a great man.

Later, when he grew up, tales were told showing how even in the first days of his life Judah HaNasi had been saved for great things. For he had been born into a well-known Jewish family. On his mother's side he was a descendant of King David. His family must have been important in the affairs of the Jews at that time because they were known to high Roman officials. These officials even reported the birth of the child to Rome, and they also reported that his parents were secretly following Jewish customs.

The story tells us that Judah's parents were ordered to Rome to appear before the Emperor, and that Judah was saved only because his mother pleaded with the Empress. The Empress, too, had a new-born son named Antoninus, and with the sympathy of one mother for another, she persuaded the Emperor to let the Jewish child live.

Strangely enough, the two boys grew up to be friends, and stories are told of how Antoninus, when he became Emperor, would visit the great Rabbi Judah HaNasi, and learn about Jewish law and wisdom from him.

While Judah was growing up, he studied in the city of Usha. Rabbi Meir was head of the school. And so it was there that Judah took up the unfinished task of the chain of rabbis in arranging all the Jewish laws. In his turn, Judah became a rabbi, and a member of the Sanhedrin, which was still meeting, even though it was no longer in Jerusalem.

Like Hillel, Judah became head of the Sanhedrin and received the title of Nasi, or Prince, which was the highest honor among the Jews.

Befriending a Roman emperor

Because of his high position, he spoke on behalf of the Jews to the Romans, and he had to make visits to the city of the Roman Emperor. Fortunately his family had been quite rich, so Rabbi Judah HaNasi was wealthy; he used his

Judah's mother pleads for her son's life

125

wealth to provide for the brightest students of the Torah. He gathered them about him and supported them at his own cost.

It was said that when he lived near the Emperor, in the city of Sepphoris, the Roman ruler had a tunnel dug between his palace and the home of the Jewish sage so that he could secretly visit the rabbi and learn from him. And a story has come down to us about one of these visits, which took place on the Sabbath.

Rabbi Judah HaNasi invited the Emperor to the Sabbath meal, which was a cold one. But the Emperor enjoyed all the cold dishes, and praised their taste. Soon afterward the rabbi invited the Emperor to supper on a weekday. This time the food was warm, and also very well prepared, but the Emperor did not enjoy it as much. "Tell me," he said to the rabbi, "what spices were used in the dishes the other time? For even though they were cold, I found them marvelously tasty."

"Ah," said the Rabbi, "there was a special flavor from a spice that I unfortunately cannot provide today."

"Tell me what it was," said the Emperor, "and if you do not have it in your house, I will send to the palace for it, for we have every sort of spice in the palace."

"I am sure that you could not provide this one," said the rabbi, smiling, to the Emperor. "For it was the flavor of our Sabbath, which you shared with us in the cold meal and found so rare and enjoyable."

Another story told of Rabbi Judah

HaNasi is of the time when he received a gift from a non-Jew. It was a very valuable pearl. In return he sent his friend a Mezuzah. When they met again, the friend let the rabbi understand that he thought the return gift was of small value—a simple little box with a bit of parchment in it. "Ah," said the Rabbi, "but it is more precious than any of our possessions, yours or mine. For our possessions, such as the pearl you sent me, must be guarded by the owners. But the gift that I sent you, the Mezuzah, will guard the owner."

Judah HaNasi entertains a Roman emperor

Stories with a moral

As he was a pupil of the great Rabbi Meir, who was so famous for his story-telling, it is not surprising that Rabbi Judah HaNasi, too, is famous for telling stories with a moral. And just as Rabbi Meir told a famous story about fruits in a garden, so did Rabbi Judah HaNasi. He told it to his friend, the Emperor, who liked to ask him puzzling questions.

Once the Emperor asked the Rabbi-Prince a question about how sins were judged. In the future world, said the Emperor, couldn't a wicked person claim that his sins were committed by his body? And as the person would then be a soul without a body, couldn't he say that he should not be held guilty for the sins of his body?

The rabbi answered with a story. It is again a story of a garden filled with wonderful fruit. It belonged to a king. The fruit was tempting, even to the guards who were set to watch it. So the king had a bright thought. He placed a lame man and a blind man in the garden, as guards. The lame man could not climb the trees, and the blind man could not see the fruit.

But finally, tempted by the smell of the fruit, the blind man also had a bright thought. He lifted the lame man up on his shoulders so he could thus pick fruit for both of them.

When the king came to the garden, he saw that some of the finest fruit was gone. Each of the guards said he could not have taken the fruit by himself. But the king saw what had happened, and he had the blind man lift the lame man up on his shoulders so they could be judged and punished as one man. "So it is with man's body and his soul," the rabbi told the Emperor. "They cannot be judged separately from each other."

The Rabbi's wise teaching explains one of the main ideas in Jewish law, for in our story of Creation, God created man as one being, body and spirit together. And the story that the Rabbi told showed that when we do wrong, we must not try to slip out of our responsibility.

This tale helps us to see how closely story-telling could be connected with knowledge of the Law. For though Rabbi Judah HaNasi, like Rabbi Meir, knew many stories, they sprang from his great knowledge of the Law. For, as you have learned, he was busy all his life putting down our laws in orderly fashion. In this he was helped by many other rabbis, as well as by the great rabbis who had worked before him. But the Mishnah, or book of laws, was so important that Rabbi Judah HaNasi was called the greatest of all the rabbis, for having finished it. That was why, as we have said, he was sometimes simply called "The Rabbi." And even today, when scholars speak of "Rabbi," they mean Judah HaNasi, the Rabbi of Rabbis.

How Judah HaNasi simplified the Law

It was very important to have the laws put into a code at this time, when Palestine was so poor that Jews were escaping to other countries. For as they became scattered in other lands, they could take the entire Law with them, just as the Jews who first went to Babylon had taken the first scrolls of the Bible.

The laws in the Mishnah were arranged under special headings. You will see from the names of some of these books of the Mishnah how Judah Ha-Nasi made it simple for the Jews to follow their laws.

1. *Seeds*. In this book he put the rules about the share of the crop to be given to the priests, Levites, and to the poor. And he put in all the blessings and prayers for good crops, as well as other blessings.

2. *Festivals*. This book contains the rules about Sabbath, and Shavuoth, Passover, the Day of Atonement, Rosh Hashanah, Purim, and many of the less important holidays.

3. *Women*. The laws of marriage and of divorce, and the rules about family life, all go under this heading, for woman meant the home.

4. *Damages*. Here are the laws for conducting trials, which are followed to this day in the orthodox Jewish courts. The penalties for worshipping idols are also given. And an unusual part of this book is the Pirke Aboth, or the "sayings of the fathers." These are wise sayings of famous rabbis. And this is an example of how the Mishnah comes right into our lives today, for you can find the same sayings of the fathers in the prayer book, to be read at the Sabbath afternoon service.

5. *Holy Things*. The rules about sacrifice are here, even though we do not use them any more, since we do not make sacrifices. The rules of Temple worship are in this book. And there are

The six books of the Mishnah

also the rules about kosher meat which are still used by people who observe these laws today.

6. *Purification.* These are rules for cleanliness, and rules for special ritual baths for the priests and worshippers at the Temple, who had to purify themselves at certain times.

The Mishnah tells us many things about the way Jews lived in the old days. And it tells us about the beginning of Jewish worship. So that in our synagogue of today we follow many things that were being done in the time of the Rabbi of Rabbis.

It had taken a chain of generations of great rabbis to complete the Mishnah. But there is even a greater book than the Mishnah, and this is the Talmud. The Mishnah was the beginning of the Talmud. And it took three hundred years more, in two great colleges of Jerusalem and Babylon, to finish the Talmud.

THINKING ABOUT WHAT YOU HAVE LEARNED

1. What is a legend that tells how one great Rabbi is connected to the great Rabbi of the next generation?
2. How far back did Judah HaNasi trace his family history?

PARENTS

1. Tell your parents Judah HaNasi's story about the blind man and the lame man. Ask them if they have heard stories in which one person blames another for doing the wrong thing but where both are equally responsible.
2. Show your parents the section in the prayerbook containing the ''Pirke Aboth.'' Ask them to choose their favorite saying.

How the Mishnah grew into the Talmud

A thousand rabbis worked a thousand years

ONE THING WE KNOW about knowledge is that there is no end to it. So when the great chain of rabbis had arranged the rules of Jewish life in the Mishnah, it was not really the end. For they went on with an even greater work called the Gemorah. These two works together are called the Talmud. It is said that a thousand rabbis worked a thousand years to make the Talmud.

The word Talmud comes from the Hebrew word *lomed,* which means to study. A pupil, in Hebrew, is called a *talmid,* or a student. In the old days, parents used to call their sons affectionately by this name. "He is my little *talmid,*" meant that a boy was a good student.

So Talmud really means all learning. It is a collection of all Jewish learning, like an encyclopedia. And this collection was made by the rabbis in Jerusalem, and also by the rabbis in Babylonia. Why in Babylonia?

You remember that many Jews did not leave Babylonia in the time of Ezra the Scribe. They continued to live there, and built homes, and built schools, just as we do in America today. And they had some of the best schools of the Torah; one was in Sura, and one was in Pumbeditha. In these two schools, generation after generation of scholars collected the wise sayings of rabbis about the laws.

When the book of regulations, called the Mishnah, was finished, there were many discussions, just as there are discussions about any set of rules. For instance, take a very important rule, such as the one which forbade the kindling of lights on the Sabbath. Did this mean they might be kindled by a non-Jew? And that the Jew could make use of the warmth from such a fire? One rabbi would say, "yes," and another rabbi would say, "yes, but."

Scholars began to write down these discussions about the rules in the Mishnah. They would put down the points made by one rabbi in his argument, and the points made by another, and then a third rabbi might sum up the discussion. Or a fourth, or a fifth.

They would remember and write down what Hillel said, and perhaps a tale told by Rabbi Meir to show the meaning of the rule. So the Talmud contained all the rules that were in the Mishnah, and all the discussions, like embroidery around the rules.

A book of all knowledge

Some of the stories we have been reading about in the lives of the great rabbis come right out of the Talmud. For where else would they have been kept for us? It is from the Talmud that we learn about the underground tunnel used by the Emperor Antoninus, to come and visit Rabbi Judah HaNasi. And the Talmud even tells us the things they talked about, the arguments and discussions about the body and soul.

It is from the Talmud that we learn the stories of Rabbi Meir about the fox and the fruit. It is from the Talmud that we learn the love story of Rabbi Akiba, and the Golden Rule of Rabbi Hillel about not doing to others what you would not have them do to you.

And so the Talmud contained all the wisdom of our ancient people in the ancient lands. It even contained other subjects like geography and astronomy. To explain the calendar for counting the days to the holidays, the ancient rabbis would have to explain what was known about astronomy. To explain the laws about owning land, they would have to explain about seeds and crops and agriculture. They would have to explain many things about plants and animals, so that a great deal of science came into the Talmud.

The Talmud was written in two places, because of the rivalry between the academies of Jerusalem and the academies of Babylon. And also because the customs might be different in each country. But there was not a very great difference in the main rules. For the scholars went back and forth, from one country to the other.

The Talmud of Jerusalem was finished two hundred years sooner than the Talmud of Babylonia, and it is a good deal shorter. Today our scholars study both the Jerusalem Talmud and the Babylonian Talmud.

The Talmudic Rabbis arrange the calendar

But we must not think that only the scholars living in Jerusalem or Babylonia took part in making this great book of Jewish knowledge. For during that time the Jews had already become scattered in many countries, and travelers carried letters back and forth. A great rabbi in Egypt might write his thoughts to a rabbi in Jerusalem. A rabbi in Syria might send his ideas to the academy in Babylonia. That was how hundreds of rabbis took part in making the Talmud. Not everything was put in, of course. In each of the great academies, groups of rabbis decided what was important enough to put into the Talmud.

When we say it took a thousand years to make the Talmud, we mean that it began even before the Mishnah was begun, for the Mishnah is really part of it. It began when Ezra the Scribe, and other scribes, were holding discussions in Babylonia, after the First Temple was torn down. And it went on until long after the Second Temple was torn down.

Many different communities

It went on in Babylonia and in Jerusalem and in Egypt, and in Syria and in Rome and in Greece. You may wonder, how did Jewish communities come to be in all those places?

You remember they had been driven from Palestine many times by famine and by war. Sometimes they fled to Egypt. Sometimes they went the other way, to Syria or Persia. But the worst time was after the Romans destroyed the Second Temple. Then the Jews had to flee in every direction, some to Egypt, some to Babylonia, and some were car-

ried across the sea to Rome as slaves. And from Rome some escaped to other countries in Europe.

And wherever a few Jewish families gathered, they had services, for as you know, ten men were enough to hold services, with or without a rabbi. When things went well for the Jews and they found a country where they were allowed to work and to worship, they would write to their relatives and friends in other countries where Jews were not as well off. So more Jews would come to the better place. And when a good-sized community of Jews had gathered, they would build a synagogue and a place of study, where children learned the Torah, and where scholars pored over the Mishnah.

No matter in what country they lived, if they had money the Jews would send help to scholars who were still in Jerusalem, to help support the synagogues there. For Jerusalem had become a very poor city.

When the Romans beat down the last revolt of the Jews, which had been led by Bar Kochba, some scholars, as we know, fled to the hills and hid. Others fled back to Babylonia, where they had friends or relatives, or where they at least knew that there were Jewish academies. For in Babylonia the Jews had become farmers and merchants and craftsmen, and during those hundreds of years the Jewish communities had done well.

They were not always without trouble; that depended on the particular king or caliph who ruled. Still, the Babylonians had learned that the Jews were very use-

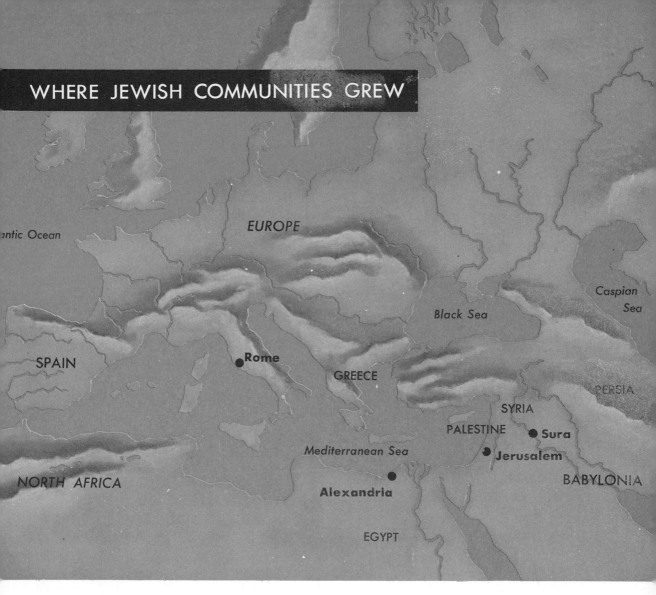

ful as traders, because many Jews went back and forth to Palestine and even to Egypt. Some of these travelers kept in touch with the scholars in all the different Jewish communities in the different lands. Thus, when things went badly in Jerusalem, teachers and students were helped to come to Babylonia. In the same way, when there was such great

trouble for the Jews of Europe in the last war many scholars and teachers from the colleges of Europe were helped to come to America.

The schools of Babylon

You can see how the chain of Jewish knowledge held together by following a pupil of the Rabbi Prince, Judah Ha- *133*

Nasi. One of his best pupils came to Palestine from Babylonia, and then went back to Babylonia to become the founder of a new academy, which became the most important one in that land. His name was Rab, and he wrote the prayer called ''Alenu L'Shabeach,'' which was so beautiful that we still recite it at the end of every service.

In the time of Rab, the Jewish community of Babylonia was flourishing, so the academies were busy with scholars working on the Talmud. And there was a great deal of interest in the communities in what the scholars were doing. Everyone liked to join in the discussions of the laws, and to show how much he knew—to show what famous sayings of the rabbis he could quote.

Our great rabbis had some wise and beautiful sayings about prayer. Here are some of them:

Prayer is Israel's only weapon. Prayer is Israel's chief joy.

A man should always think of his community when praying, ''May it be Thy will *Our* God to conduct *us* in peace.''

Prayer is greater than sacrifice or good deeds. There was no one greater in good deeds than Moses, yet his wish to see the Promised Land was secured only through prayer.

These are sayings about the synagogue as a House of Prayer, a Beth Hatifila.

And here are some of the wise sayings of the rabbis about the Beth Hamidrash, the House of Study, and about the Torah:

134 He who does not add to his learning, lessens it.

He who honors the Torah will be honored by mankind.

Study the Torah for its own sake and not in the hope of a reward.

Women are honored by sending their children to learn the Torah in the synagogue.

God created the Torah before He created the world, and consulted the Torah as a plan.

Kallah — a school for adults in Babylon

When we read these sayings and see how the great rabbis felt about the Torah, we understand why teaching the Torah in our religious schools is so important. In the old days, the Jews of Babylonia were so keenly interested that they started classes to learn from the Talmud. Twice a year, after the harvest, they would gather in special schools where they studied for a month at a time. Their scholars would gather first, in the academy, to discuss all the new laws. This great meeting was called a Kallah. Then when they returned to their villages, they would explain the Kallah. It was like what we call "adult education" nowadays, when your parents and other grown-ups come to a lecture course in the synagogue. So you see we have much in common with the Jews of Babylonia who lived hundreds of years ago.

Along the Mediterranean

But Babylonia was not the only great Jewish community that grew up outside of Palestine. As Jewish families grew, and as Jewish traders moved on from one country to another to earn their living, Jewish communities sprang up. If you will look at the map, you will see that the first great Jewish communities were around the Mediterranean Sea. When we looked at this map before, we saw that different countries around the Mediterranean Sea took turns in becoming strong. Each would take a turn in conquering the other lands around the seacoast. And we saw that many of these conquerors passed through Judea, which was later called Palestine.

They took Jews away as slaves. But sometimes these slaves were freed in the new land, and they settled there to live and to start a Jewish community as Jews had done in Babylonia. Or sometimes, Jews who fled along the seacoast found a place to settle, and started a community. Jews moved from Palestine to Egypt, and from Egypt along the coast to many other places in North Africa. Casablanca is such a place. If you will look at the map, you will notice that the sea becomes very narrow between North Africa and Spain. So the Jews moved across to Spain.

Then they moved to other lands in Europe. But wherever they went, they had a house of study and a synagogue. And they handed down their Torah and later their Talmud from father to son.

And you will see how we can follow the path of our ancestors, through their synagogues.

THINKING ABOUT WHAT YOU HAVE LEARNED

1. Why is the Talmud compared to an encyclopedia? How is it different?
2. How did the Kallah help people learn about the Talmud?

PARENTS

1. Ask your parents to tell you about the Adult Education program of your congregation.
2. Can America be called a "Center" of Judaism as Babylonia was in Talmudic times?

A Roman galley in the Mediterranean Sea

How the Synagogue grew and spread to every land

CHAPTER XXIII

What ancient synagogues were like

JUST AS OUR OWN synagogue belongs to us, all the synagogues of long ago belong to us, because they are part of the story of our people and our religion. By studying the books that were read and studied in those synagogues, and by finding all that is left of those synagogues as far back as we can go, we find out more about ourselves. It is like looking for old family photographs and letters and mementos. But this is even more important, because these ancient stones that tell us of our worship, tell us how we came to know God.

We can begin with the stones and the scriptures that have been found in Palestine, and the countries near Palestine, around the Mediterranean Sea. Later, as the Jews moved further away, we can follow them by their schools and their synagogues, up to our own time.

When we find the ruins of ancient synagogues, they make us think of one important fact. We find ruins of other religious temples, from the same time as the oldest synagogue. We know of the beautiful ruins of Greek Temples,

and of the pyramids and tombs where the Egyptians worshipped their dead kings. Yet those religions are no longer alive. The Greeks of today do not worship the famous Greek gods about whom their stories were told. And the Egyptians of today are mostly Arabs of the Moslem religion, which is nothing like the ancient Egyptian religion.

Yet when we find the oldest Jewish scrolls, where they were hidden away in caves in Palestine, we find that they are the same, word for word, as our Torah of today. The scrolls that were read in the synagogues in the time of Rabbi Hillel, and surely before, are the scrolls that we read in our synagogue. The same words are printed in our Bible.

When the Romans were worshipping their mad Emperor Caligula, and long before when the Greeks were worshipping Zeus, and Artemis, and so many other gods, the Jews were worshipping the One God. They said, His name cannot be said, for God is too great for humans to give Him a name.

The Jews have stayed together because they studied in order to know God, and today part of our study is our past. We want to retrace our steps into the past, and we can do so by looking at what we have found of the ancient synagogues.

The words were copied down

You may wonder how we know what happened in the synagogues so long ago. There were no photographs in those days, so we have no pictures of exactly what they looked like. And there were no drawings on the ancient scrolls. But the words help us.

The Bible tells us exactly what the first Ark looked like, and later, it tells about the Temple of Solomon, and even later, about the Second Temple. By the time the Romans ruined the Second Temple, centuries had passed, and more

people had learned how to write, and some of them were writing histories. A man named Josephus, who lived during the war with the Romans, wrote a very long history about these days. When you grow up, you may study Josephus.

You may wonder if we have the original scrolls that were written by hand for the first synagogue. These have been lost. But as a scroll grew old, copies were made, and so we have copies of copies of copies.

The scrolls of the Bible were translated, because the Jews moved from one country to another, and used the language of each country. Until a few years ago, the very oldest scrolls that people had found were those in the Greek translation.

But in 1947 some shepherds in Palestine found some scrolls that were in jars in a cave, near the Dead Sea. A famous Israeli scholar, Professor Eleazer Sukenik of the Hebrew University, figured out that these scrolls were the oldest that had ever been found Other scholars agree that they come from the time of Rabbi Hillel! And in these scrolls the words of the prophets proved to be exactly the same as we have them in the Bible today.

Finding the Dead Sea Scrolls

Professor Sukenik was a great archaeologist. An archaeologist is someone who studies the records of how human beings lived long, long ago. These records are found in caves and in ruins; sometimes they are arrowheads or bronze knives or stone hammers. So you see that archaeology is a good deal like detective work. We are now able to prove that the Bible has come down to us exactly as it was in the ancient scrolls, word for word, and that the translations were correct, too.

Because the Bible was holy, great care was taken when translations were made. There is a famous legend about the first time the Bible was translated into Greek. This was at the time when many Jews had fled from Palestine, and were living in Alexandria. If you will look on your map, you will see that Alexandria is on the coast of Egypt, and this may puzzle you. For why were Jews talking Greek in Egypt?

Unfortunately, history is complicated. The Greeks had conquered Egypt and built a city where Greek was spoken. A very large Jewish colony grew up in this city of Alexandria, because it was the nearest city the Jews could flee to when things were bad in Palestine. And the Greek ruler became interested in Jewish worship. He heard about their holy books. And he decided to have the Bible translated into the Greek language. So he sent to Jerusalem for seventy scholars; he put them on a small island, each one in a different room, and had each one make a separate translation. When they were all finished, the seventy translations were compared, and they were all exactly the same, word for word! So from this story we always believed that the translations that have come down to us were exactly right. Now the archaeologists are proving this. And the archaeologists are helping us to find out things that were not even written down in the scrolls, as well as to prove that things that were written about really happened. For instance, when the Bible speaks of Solomon's stables, we can now prove the description is true, because the places where his horses were stabled have been dug out.

How we know about history

Have you ever watched a building being built, and seen how the foundations are dug? And have you wondered if the diggers will find ancient coins or arrows in the foundation hole? Have you wondered who might have lived on the same spot, long ago? That is archaeology. Have you ever gone camping, and picked a good spot to camp, only to discover signs that someone had camped and built a fire there before? If a place is close to water, or if it has good protection, other people before you

Things archaeologists may find

140

will have had the idea that it is a good place to camp or to live.

The same way with ancient towns. Some of the towns where people lived thousands of years ago were covered with sand and earth when disasters wiped out the people or when an enemy burned their city. Archaeologists have dug up ruins of such towns in Palestine. They have investigated the caves where our ancestors lived, as far back as Abraham. They have found where they cooked, and spots where the ancient altars of worship once stood. They have found old coins from the days of the Maccabees, and weapons, and pieces of pottery, and pieces of baked clay with strange writings on them. In other lands, in Egypt and Babylonia, they have found things that show how people lived in the days of Abraham and Moses.

A favorite digging place for archaeologists is Palestine. Many places still have the same names we find in the Bible. If an archaeologist sees a certain kind of mound, and it has a biblical name, then he knows it should be a good place to dig. You may travel to Israel one day and see these strange mounds. What are they? They are layers and layers of towns!

One of the famous archaeologists who dug up important places in Palestine is an American. His name is Dr. Nelson Glueck. It was he, for example, who discovered the location of King Solomon's copper mines. And now, modern Israelis are digging in these mines, just where King Solomon's miners left off.

If you watch the newspapers, you will read from time to time of new discoveries made by archaeologists in Israel. Sometimes it does not take scientists to make these discoveries. The new settlers of Israel may be digging a well, or digging the foundation of a house, when they come upon ancient relics. That is one of the excitements of living in such an historic country.

Suppose two thousand years from now, when you will have had great-great-great-grandchildren, an archaeologist starts digging to uncover the cities of today. And suppose he finds a bronze plaque with something printed on it. It may read, "In Memory of Mr. and Mrs. Joseph Cohen who generously donated the funds to help build this synagogue and school, for the study of the Torah and the teaching of God's Law."

141

Then he might figure out what the synagogue was like, and what our life was like.

We do the same with messages left by our great-great-great-grandparents in Israel. For among the ruins uncovered by the archaeologists in Palestine are the remains of more than forty synagogues. One of these goes back to the days of the Second Temple. There is even an inscribed stone which says, "Theodotus built this synagogue for the reading of the Law and the teaching of the Commandments."

Now let us see what we can learn from this message. The name is not a Hebrew name. Theodotus is a Greek name. Remember about the rich men in the time of the Second Temple who wanted to imitate the Greeks? Then here is a Jew whose family adopted a Greek name. But still he remained a good Jew and gave money to build a synagogue. And what was done in the synagogue? The stone tells us they read out the Law, as we do in our services today. And they taught, as we do in our schools.

How strange it is to find relics that show us that the people of those times were very much as we are today.

We find beauty in ancient ruins

One of the most famous and most beautiful synagogue ruins in Israel is on the shores of the Sea of Galilee, at a place called Capernaum. If you visit Israel, you will surely want to go there. You can reach these ruins by a lovely boat-trip on the lake. The floor is still there, and there are bits of walls and columns still standing, and from these clues artists have made drawings to show what the synagogue looked like when it was in use. This was a large synagogue, and it was decorated with beautiful mosaics—designs made with little pieces of colored stone.

The Synagogue at Capernaum was in use at the time when the Romans conquered Palestine. The town of Capernaum is mentioned in the books written by Josephus.

Another early synagogue, from the same century, has been found at Kfar Birim. But the oldest synagogue ruins that have been discovered so far are not in Palestine. They are in the city of Alexandria, in Egypt. A piece of stone was found among the ruins saying that it was built during the reign of King Ptolemy II. At that time, the Second Temple was still standing in Jerusalem. You may wonder, how was a synagogue of those days different from the Temple in Jerusalem?

A synagogue at Capernaum

Reconstruction of an ancient synagogue

The very first houses of worship

The Temple was mostly an open court-yard where the priests could make sacrifices. There was a place called the Holy of Holies, which only the high priests could enter.

But a synagogue has always been a place where everybody could enter. The early synagogues that have been found in Palestine had a wide center aisle, with pillars on both sides to hold up the balcony. And there were two side aisles, almost like a modern theatre. In some synagogues diggers have found a rounded space, or niche, where the Ark could be kept. We even know how those synagogues looked, from pictures found on old coins, or even on old pieces of glass. Ancient drinking glasses have been found, with pictures painted on the bottom.

In an ancient synagogue near Tiberias, in Palestine, a stone Menorah was found! Pictures of Menorahs also have been found on coins and on glass. Judging by the shape of the Menorahs in these pictures, some experts say that they were made not out of stone but out of metal, as they are today.

Ruins of ancient synagogues have been found not only in Egypt and in Palestine, but in Syria, the country on the other side of Palestine. In one of the Syrian synagogues, called Dura-Europos, a stone Bimah was discovered. This is the platform on which the Torah was unrolled to be read to the congregation, just as it is today.

In other synagogues the Bimah was probably made of wood, which has rotted away. This may explain why no more such reading platforms have been found.

In these ancient synagogues the people sat on stone benches which were lined against the side walls. The most important seat was called the Seat of Moses. This was surely for the leader

143

Mosaic used to decorate an ancient synagogue

of the congregation. The benches were reserved for the important men, the elders. And the rest of the worshippers, except for the women, probably sat on the floor. The women sat in the balcony, as they were to do in all synagogues for many centuries, for it was the custom to separate women from men during worship. In the Temple in Jerusalem there was a special courtyard for women.

People usually want to make their places of worship beautiful, and that is why some of the most beautiful buildings in the world are synagogues, and churches, and mosques, and temples of all kinds.

Beauty in the synagogue

One thing about the ancient synagogues found in Palestine and other countries was surprising. To make them more beautiful, they were often decorated with pictures of people and ani-

mals. These decorations were mosaics of colored stones or bits of glass, on the floors and walls. Sometimes, too, there were traces of paintings. And there were stone carvings among the ruins.

Now, why should this have been surprising?

Because the diggers remembered, just as we remembered, that the second of the Ten Commandments tells us not to make graven images. The Bible says not to make any manner of likeness of anything that is in the heaven above, or that is in the earth beneath, or that is in the water.

We all know this commandment was made to stop idol worship. When all the people around the Jews worshipped idols of animals, it was hard for some Jews not to do the same. You remember how even while Moses was up on Mount Sinai receiving the Ten Commandments, some of the superstitious people made a Golden Calf and worshipped it.

The Egyptians and the Hittites and the Amorites and the Babylonians all worshipped gods of clay and stone, shaped like people, or like bulls, or snakes, or eagles. The Romans worshipped statues of their own emperors as though they were gods. So our prophets and our priests and our rabbis had always to remind the Jews that God cannot be seen or imagined.

But when the Jews were no longer in danger of forgetting this, the rabbis decided that it was not wrong for them to make beautiful designs of people and flowers and animals. For they would not mistake them for gods and worship them. They would see in them only the

144

Uncovering a wall painting in an ancient synagogue

beautiful handiwork of God.

And therefore permission was given to decorate the synagogues. For our greatest rabbis have always taught us that the Jewish religion must grow as our understanding grows.

So even in some of the early synagogues we find pictures and statues. People as well as animals are shown, but of course they are not idols. Sometimes the images are symbols.

For example, a lion is a symbol of strength. And the lion is the symbol of the tribe of Judah. On the site of an ancient synagogue in the town of Chorazin, a stone lion was found, which the archaeologists believed was one of two lions, guarding each side of the Ark. Many of our synagogues today have the Lion of Judah on each side of the doors of the Ark.

And in some of the oldest synagogues that have been dug up, beautiful pictures and decorations of all kinds have been found. The most famous are the wall paintings in that same synagogue in Syria, Dura-Europos. These pictures were covered for hundreds of years because the synagogue was built right against the town wall. And once when there was a war, and the Persians were attacking the Syrians, the wall was made thicker for protection. When the wall was made thicker, the pictures were covered up.

Centuries later, part of the brick and clay fell away, and people saw the paintings underneath. Scientists came, and carefully uncovered the old wall of the synagogue of Dura-Europos. The pictures on this wall tell us a series of stories just like cartoon strips in a newspaper of today.

The most interesting pictures show the story of the Prophet Ezekiel, and the valley of the dry bones. At the left is the Hand of God showing Ezekiel his way through the valley of dry bones. *145*

On the right, the Hand of God shows Ezekiel the prophecy that the bones shall rise and become human beings once more.

Other pictures show a prophet with a scroll of the Law, and this may be Moses, or Ezra the Scribe. They show Jacob, Moses, Aaron, Joshua, and Elijah, and illustrate the story of Purim.

The synagogue at Dura-Europos is one of the very few places where the decorations were painted pictures. In most synagogues of the early days, the decorations were mosaics, just as in many churches that were built at the same period.

One reason for choosing mosaics may have been because people, knowing that religion deals with eternal matters, wanted their places of worship to last forever. So they made pictures out of bits of stone, and they have lasted for centuries.

In modern Israel, for instance, when the settlers of the colony of Beth Alpha were digging ditches in which to lay their water piping, they came upon some ancient ruins. They fenced off the area, and sent a message to Professor Sukenik in Jerusalem. He came to Beth Alpha and supervised the diggers as they un-covered the remains of a synagogue that was built fourteen hundred years ago.

The floor of this synagogue was all mosaic. Thousands and thousands of bits of stone of beautiful colors were arranged to make pictures. The top panels showed the Ark, the Eternal Light, the Menorah, the Lions of Judah, the Shofar, and other ceremonial objects, many of them the same as we use in our synagogues today. In the center were the signs of the Zodiac, the star-system used by astrologers. On the bottom panel was a picture story of Abraham and Isaac. Hebrew and Greek inscriptions were on the panels, just as we may have Hebrew and English in our synagogues today.

So you see how our synagogue has lived for many, many years. Today, as in the days of Beth Alpha and Dura-Europos, we try to make our synagogues beautiful, with sculptures, mural paintings, stained glass windows, and mosaics by some of our best artists. But a humble and plain synagogue also contains the beauty of the spirit.

You will see now how the synagogue, through this spirit, came to live in so many far and different places in the world.

THINKING ABOUT WHAT YOU HAVE LEARNED

1. How do we know what the earliest synagogues looked like?
2. Many people have wondered why synagogues have very little art compared to the buildings of other religions. What reason is usually given for this?

PARENTS

1. What are the oldest records your parents have of your family history?
2. What kind of art would your parents like to see in your synagogue?

CHAPTER XXIV

From Babylon to Spain

WHEN PEOPLE TRAVEL to different places in the world, they love to look at ruins. When you grow up you may visit the beautiful country of Greece, across the sea from Israel. In Greece is the beautiful city of Athens, named for one of the early Greek goddesses, Athena. And in the city of Athens, on top of a hill, are the ruins of beautiful temples of worship where sacrifices were made to the Greek gods and goddesses of olden times.

Greece is still a country of Greeks, but they do not worship these gods; and they look upon the ruins of their temples only to remind themselves of their times of ancient power and splendor.

But in Greece and in other lands you will also find Jews. And you will find synagogues where our services are read —the same services that began in Jerusalem before the time of the Greeks.

As you know, Jews settled in Greece and in other countries when they were driven from Palestine. They moved further and further in order to earn their living. There came the years known as the Dark Ages, when there was a great deal of fighting in Europe. The Dark Ages came after the Roman Empire was destroyed by barbarians who came down from the North.

The Romans had ruled other lands; they had ruled in Palestine and other countries around the coast of the Mediterranean Sea. Now there were wars and troubles in those lands. The Jews moved, to get away from the troubles. They started new communities in places like Spain. In these new communities they often had no rabbis, for the community would be quite small at the beginning. Sometimes these Jews were not sure of the rules of worship. So they would write to the famous rabbis still living in Jerusalem, or in Babylonia, for advice. We even have some of these ancient letters.

Letters were sent from land to land

From the early letters of scattered Jews, and from the answers of the great rabbis in Jerusalem and Babylon, we can get a very good idea of how the Jews lived and worshipped in those times. Such letters give us more of an idea than we get from digging up stone ruins. And so we know even more about those days. In fact, much of our prayer book   *147*

comes from those days, because it was in answer to such a letter that the first prayer book was put together.

The letter came from the Jews of Spain to Rabbi Amram, who was the head of the Talmudic college in the Babylonian city named Sura. As we know, this was a very famous college, where most of the Babylonian Talmud was written.

Of course there was no regular mail. The Spanish Jews sent the letter by a traveler who was going to North Africa. He gave it to another traveler who was going to Jerusalem. And that traveler found a good Jew who was going to Babylonia, and who carried the letter to Sura. The letter asked which prayers should be recited at the services.

From the fact that it was sent to Babylonia, we know that in those days the community of Jews in Babylonia was the most important to the Jews all over the world. More Jews were living there than in Palestine, which had been laid waste by so many wars. And the community of Jews in Babylonia was very well organized.

Princes in exile

The Jews of Babylonia even had a leader who was known as the Prince of Exile, or the Exilarch. He was called by this name because the Jews still thought of themselves as being in exile from their home in Palestine. He sat on a kind of throne in the greatest synagogue of Bagdad. You may know of Bagdad from the famous tales of Caliphs in the "Arabian Nights." These Caliphs ruled in the city and in the country around Bagdad at about the same time

148

as the Exilarchs.

On the right hand of the Exilarch, on great official occasions, sat the head of the Academy of Sura. On his left hand sat the head of the Academy of Pumbaditha. These great scholars were not only like the presidents of colleges today. They were also judges, for they decided what was correct in Jewish law. You might say that the head of the academy of Sura was like a Chief Justice of the Supreme Court.

Why was Sura so important? You remember how the torch of learning was carried from one country to another. You remember that this great academy of Sura was started by a scholar named Rab, who came from Jerusalem in the bad years after the Romans ruined Palestine. And Rab himself took the torch of learning from the hands of the Rabbi of Rabbis, Judah HaNasi, who completed the Mishnah.

Then Rab carried his learning to Babylonia and started the college of Sura. Many years later, the head of the college of Sura wrote a prayer book to answer the request from Jews who lived far away in Spain.

Some Jews, like those of Spain, sent letters to Babylonia asking their questions about worship. And some Jews, who were scholars in distant lands, made the voyage to Babylonia.

Another wise and famous rabbi

One was a young scholar named Saadya. He was born in Egypt. Even before he was twenty-one, Saadya was famous in the Egyptian city of Alexandria, where Jews had lived for centuries. He wrote a book explaining the festivals, and it was filled with brilliance and wisdom.

After that, Saadya went to Jerusalem to keep on with his studies, for there were still academies of the Talmud in Jerusalem, even though the country had become very poor. And in Jerusalem Saadya became even more famous among the rabbis. He was so famous that he was called to Babylonia to settle an argument between the two great academies of Sura and Pumbaditha.

Once he was in Babylonia, the Jews did not want him to leave. Although he was still a young man, they gave him the most important place among learned men. They made him head of the Academy of Sura. A great judge of this kind was called a Gaon—a very wise man. So his name became Saadya Gaon. You know that a man of wisdom is often remembered longer than the highest official. We remember the name of Saadya Gaon today, even though the Exilarch of his time is forgotten.

Saadya settling a dispute

Saadya Gaon remained in Babylonia and wrote many books. One of them was a grammar of the Hebrew language. Another was a rhyming dictionary for poets. But his most important work was a translation of the Bible into Arabic.

The Jews who lived in Babylonia no longer spoke Hebrew in their daily life. They used Arabic, which was the language of the people around them. And when Saadya Gaon translated the Bible into Arabic, he made it easier for more people to read. Not only the Jews could read it, but Arabs could read it, and this helped them to understand their Jewish neighbors.

Thus, he did something which has been copied in many lands through the ages, for the Bible has been translated for all people to read.

An adventure with pirates

There was another custom, begun in those days, which we have with us today. This was fund-raising. You know how even children will help to collect money for a good cause, and how parents give money to support schools and hospitals in their own city and important works in Israel, North Africa, and other lands. Messengers come to us from Israel. They visit Jewish communities all over the world and tell of the work that is being done, and of the need for that work.

Just so, in the old days, when Babylonia was the center of Jewish studies, some of the great rabbis traveled to Jewish communities in other lands, to raise funds for the colleges and for Jews who were the victims of wars. One of these travelers was Rabbi Moses ben Hanoch, who had a real adventure.

Travel in those days was not easy. You couldn't get on a plane and have a nice meal served by a hostess, then get off the next morning on the other side of the world. People traveled by caravan and by ship.

There were robbers in the deserts and pirates on the seas. The pirates knew that if they captured a Jew, they could get ransom from other Jews. They happened to attack the ship on which Rabbi Moses ben Hanoch was sailing. Luckily, although they knew they had captured a Jew among their prisoners, they did not know he was a famous rabbi or they would have demanded a terribly big ransom for him. They thought he was an ordinary Jewish traveler. After many weeks, the pirate ship stopped at the Spanish port of Cordova. The chief pirate announced he had a Jew for ransom, and the Jewish community sent money to save the Jew. So Rabbi Moses ben Hanoch was free.

But he did not tell the Jews of Cordova who he was. Since they had a small college of the Talmud, he went there to visit. An argument was going

Pirates capture Jews for ransom

on about a difficult point in Talmudic law. The visitor offered his answer. The scholars were surprised, for how could a simple traveler discuss a question that had puzzled the wisest rabbis in Cordova?

But when they heard his answer, with quotations from Saadya Gaon and other famous scholars of Babylonia, they knew it was no ordinary captive they had ransomed. They knew he was a great rabbi. They begged Moses ben Hanoch to remain in Cordova, and he became head of their college. Soon the College of Cordova was as famous as the College of Sura in Babylonia.

So you see how Jewish learning spread from one land to another, even with the help of pirates.

It was an important Jew named Hasdai Ibn Shaprut who helped ransom Rabbi Moses from the pirates.

You may wonder what link you have with these people who lived so far away, so long ago, and who had such strange names, names like Shaprut. But do you know anyone named Shapiro? Some people believe such names are connected. Perhaps a Shapiro is a son of the sons of the sons of this Spanish grandee. For the Jews of Spain, when their turn came, were to wander very far.

THINKING ABOUT WHAT YOU HAVE LEARNED

1. How did Rabbi Amram happen to put together the first known Hebrew prayerbook?
2. Why was Moses ben Hanoch on a ship that was captured by pirates?

PARENTS

1. Ask your parents to tell you about the "Arabian Nights" written about the same time and in the same place where the late Rabbis in Babylon taught the Talmud.
2. What experiences have your parents had with "messengers" who came to ask for money for Jewish causes?

151

CHAPTER XXV

The Golden Age in Spain

ONE OF THE THINGS that your parents ask themselves is, "Where is the best place to raise children?" You often must have heard them discussing this. Sometimes a grown-up will get an offer of a good job in a new town, or in some country far away, and he will discuss with his wife whether it is a good place to raise children. If he has friends, or if there are other Jews there, he will write and ask them this question, and if the answer is good, he may move.

That is one reason why, in the past, Jews moved from one country to another. When things were getting bad where they lived, they would look for a better place for their children. And, about a thousand years ago, one of the best places was Spain.

The good years they had in Spain are called the Golden Age of the Jews in Spain. Because in those years Jews were free to study and to worship in their own way, and to raise their children to be good Jews.

In those years, many great colleges arose, and many Jews studied not only to become rabbis, but to become physicians and bankers. Some of them became great poets. And some of their poetry is recited by us in our synagogues today.

A Spanish rabbi

In the Golden Age of Spain, a poet and physician named Yehuda Halevi became famous. He lived in the city of Toledo. He wrote poetry in Hebrew, about love, and the beauties of nature, and the Jewish love of God, and the hopes of the Jewish people for a world of peace.

Yehuda Halevi was interested not only in the Jews of his own city, Toledo, and not only in the Jews of Spain. He wondered about the Jews all over the world. Whenever a Jewish traveler came to Toledo, the famous doctor-poet would invite him to his house and would question him about the Jews he had seen or heard about in the far places of the world.

How the Jews came to Russia

Yehuda Halevi heard about letters written by Hasdai Ibn Shaprut to a people in far off Russia, whose king had become interested in Judaism. These people were called Khazars. Some said that these people were the Ten Lost Tribes of Israel. Others told a different story about how they had become Jews. And this story was a strange one.

You know that Jews did not try to make anyone else believe in their religion. But the King of the Khazars had heard of the three great religions in the outside world. He had heard of Judaism, Christianity, and Mohammedanism. And he decided that his people ought to have a religion. So he sent for a Jew, a Christian, and a Moslem, and each had to explain his religion. When he heard that the Christians and the Moslems also believed in the Jewish Bible, he decided that he would become a Jew and that all the Khazars should be Jews.

When Dr. Yehuda Halevi heard this story, he wrote a long letter explaining all about Jewish worship. But this letter was really not a letter. It was a whole book, which he called the Kuzari. And the strangest thing of all is that if it were not for this book, which has come down to us, we would know nothing about the Khazars.

FROM SPAIN TO RUSSIA

antic Ocean

Worms

Troyes

RUSSIA

SPAIN

Toledo

Cordova

Black Sea

Mediterranean Sea

Jerusalem

NORTH AFRICA

Maimonides, physician to the Sultan

A poet-rabbi

Another great Jew of the Golden Age in Spain, who was also a poet, was Solomon ibn Gabirol. "Ibn" in Arabic means "son," just like "ben" in Hebrew. In the old days people were named that way, and you can also think of many modern names of this kind, such as Mendelson, Benson, Richardson, and Wilkinson. Other people are named after the cities and towns they came from, such as Romano and Jerushalim and Warshawsky and Berliner.

Solomon ibn Gabirol, Solomon the son of Gabriel, lived in Granada. He wrote some of the most beautiful poems that have ever been written in the Hebrew language, and you can find examples of them in the Prayer Book today. Some of them were set to music, and we sing them often at services.

Like the great doctor-poet, Yehuda Halevi, this poet also wrote books to explain Jewish customs. Solomon ibn Gabirol wrote these books in Arabic instead of in Hebrew, just as Saadya Gaon had translated the Bible into Arabic, for more people to read. When people understand each other's ideas, they are less likely to get into trouble with each other.

The "13 beliefs" of Moses Maimonides

And there was still another great writer, a doctor who was born in the Golden Age in Spain. He was born in Cordova, the same city where Rabbi Moses ben Hanoch was rescued from the pirates. He studied at the college that had been founded by Rabbi Moses. He also studied medicine, and became a famous physician. His name was Moses Maimonides.

But by the time he was ready to work at his profession, things had changed for the Jews in Cordova. The rulers were no longer friendly to the Jews. Moses Maimonides, like so many other Jews in our history, started to travel to look for a good place to live.

So you see how things go in circles in the world: Spain, which had been kind to the Jews, was growing bad, and Egypt, which had been bad to the Jews, was growing tolerant again. Moses Maimonides settled in Egypt. He became the physician of the Sultan. And Sultan Saladin also appointed him head of the Jewish community in Egypt.

Moses Maimonides had studied in the Talmudic school of Cordova, and he knew all of the laws of the Talmud. To learn all these laws, one had to read many volumes. Moses Maimonides was a man with a very orderly mind, and, like Rabbi Akiba centuries before him in Palestine, he decided to put the laws in order so it would be easier for the Jews to find a particular decision. First, as a young man of only twenty, he tried to find a simple, short way to remind Jews of their beliefs. Of course the great Rabbi Hillel had made the simplest rule, the Golden Rule, "Do not do unto others what you would not have them do unto you." And the first Moses, at Mount Sinai, had given us the Ten Commandments. Now, Moses Maimonides made a list of Thirteen Beliefs.

You may wonder why Moses Maimonides had to make a code of Thirteen Beliefs when we already had the Ten Commandments. A belief is different from a Commandment. A commandment tells us how to behave. A belief reminds us of what we hold true in our hearts about God and life. It is our faith.

For instance, Christians, or Moslems, or Jews, or people who are not religious, may ask, "Do the Jews believe in a Messiah?" And you see how faiths can be different, because Jews believe in a Messiah that is to come, and the Christians believe in a Messiah who already has come on earth.

That is why it is important to put down our great beliefs. Maimonides tried to do this, and his creed became known as the Thirteen Articles of Faith. It was made into a poem, called Yigdal, which happens to be its first word, in Hebrew. And Yigdal is still in our prayer books today. But even when he was a young scholar in Cordova, not all the Jews agreed with the way Moses Maimonides had listed our beliefs. And today, too, many Jews do not entirely agree with his list.

Maimonides went on in his Jewish studies, even while he was a famous physician, and he arranged all the laws of the Talmud in fourteen volumes. He called his great work the Mishneh Torah.

Moses Maimonides was a very great Jew. When people tried to explain how great he was, they said "From Moses to Moses there was none like Moses." Meaning he was the greatest Jew since Moses led the Jews out of Egypt.

So you see that when the Spanish Jews were a small community, they were helped to stay together by the synagogue and by the explanations of the Torah, and the rules of prayer that were sent them from Jews in other lands. When the Jews of Spain prospered, and had their own colleges, some of their great men added to our knowledge of the Torah. And they added beautiful prayers to our worship. In their turn, the Jews of Spain carried the torch of learning, which they had received from the Jews of Babylonia, who had received it from Jerusalem. Then they, too, carried it to other lands.

THINKING ABOUT WHAT YOU HAVE LEARNED

1. Why is the period when the Jews lived under Mohammedan rule in Spain known as the "Golden Age"?
2. Famous Spanish Jews of this period also helped to make their neighbors healthy and wealthy. What occupations did they have to do this?

PARENTS

1. Is our Jewish Community having a "Golden Age" now?
2. Ask your parents if they think the story of the Khazars could happen today.

CHAPTER XXVI

How a French wine-maker taught the Torah

DURING THE GOLDEN AGE of the Jews in Spain, we know that not only rabbis but poets and doctors added to our knowledge of the Torah and wrote poems for the prayer books that we use in our worship. We know that colleges grew up in Spain, to take the place of those in Babylonia, which were declining.

But what was happening in the rest of Europe? Were there Jews in other lands in Europe? You remember that even from the very old times when Jews of Palestine were captured and taken away to be slaves, there were Jews in different lands of Europe. There were Jewish communities in Rome and in Greece. Not all of them were begun by slaves who won their freedom. Some were begun by traders. And in all of them, there were synagogues to keep the Jews together.

We know, also, that there were very ancient Jewish communities in other lands such as France and Germany. We do not know exactly how they began. Perhaps scientists of future days will dig, and will find documents that tell

us more. But we already know some very interesting things about the Jews of those old times in France and Germany.

Perhaps their ancestors had traveled up the great River Rhine, as traders. Perhaps they had come around the coast of France by sea. By the year 1,000 C. E. there were already old Jewish settlements in many places in Europe. One of these places was in the wine-growing land in the northern part of France. This is the part of France where wine is now made into a famous drink—champagne. Champagne is famous because it is a fine wine that people drink on the greatest occasions, such as marriages, and college graduations, and to celebrate a birth. And because of the way champagne sparkles, we often hear people saying that a man's wisdom sparkles like champagne.

History tells us that many Jews were among the wine growers of France, where champagne now comes from. They lived near the city of Troyes.

It is not surprising that Jews were

Tending a vineyard in medieval France

good wine makers. Perhaps this knowledge was handed down in their families from far, far back, for the Bible tells us often about vineyards in Judea. One of our greatest stories, you remember, is about the prophet Elijah who went right to up King Ahab and told him he sinned when he stole Naboth's vineyard.

So two thousand years later, there were Jews who tended fine vineyards in France, and who also kept up the great chain of Jewish wisdom. To such a Jew,

named Isaac, a very bright son was born, whom he named Shlomo, or as we say it today, Solomon, after our wise king. This new Solomon became one of the most famous rabbis of the next thousand years. He is known by the name of Rashi. How did he get this name? It is made of his initials, Rabbi Shlomo, son of Isaac: Ra-Sh-I.

When he was a boy, Solomon went away to an academy of Jewish studies in a city along the Rhine river, the city of

Worms. So we know that there was already a Jewish college there in the middle of Europe, a thousand years ago, even before Germany was known as a nation. We know that there were enough Jewish communities in the middle of Europe for them to start a college of their own, for Babylonia, and even Spain were far away.

And so during the Golden Age in Spain, when some Jews were writing poems of prayer, and when Maimonides was writing his Articles of Faith, Jews in the middle of Europe were quietly studying.

Commentaries are explanations

Even while he was at the academy in Worms, Rashi became famous for his fine discussions of the Bible and the Talmud. You too, when you read a book, discuss its meaning. And the deeper and more important the book, the more we discuss it. So the Jews and other people have never stopped discussing the Bible.

Some of these discussions are sermons in the synagogue. Some of the discussions by rabbis and scholars are written down, and are called Commentaries. They are about all kinds of subjects, for the great rabbis and scholars of old times had to know about everything. We have seen that some of them were also great doctors, like Maimonides. We know that some were astronomers. And so a wise scholar like Rashi, when he writes about the Bible and the Talmud, also shows us that he knows many things about history and medicine and mathematics.

A page of an early printed Hebrew book

The commentaries that Rashi wrote to explain the Bible were so important that they were the first books printed in Hebrew, when printing was invented hundreds of years later.

And if you want to see how important Rashi was, you have only to look at a page of the printed Talmud. You will see that the main part is printed in the middle, and then there is another part printed all around it like a frame. This frame is made up of the commentaries of great rabbis. Any student will sometimes write notes on the margin of a page he is reading. He will write down what he thinks of what he reads. He may start an argument about what he is reading, or he may add an idea that proves that what he is reading is right.

Our great rabbis did this with the Talmud. The best of these commentaries are printed around the pages. And the one that is used most is the commentary of Rashi.

You can see how wise he was by one story. Besides writing his long commentaries on the many long books of the Talmud, Rashi answered hundreds of letters from other rabbis, and from ordinary Jews, about points of law. Very often he wrote "I don't know." It is a wise man who admits what he doesn't know.

The story of Rashi and the monk

Besides writing his commentaries on the Bible and the Talmud, Rashi kept up the ancient Jewish custom of earning his living outside of his studies. He had come back to his family home in Troyes to live, after he was married, and he cultivated the family vineyards. He was the Rabbi of Troyes.

But he also traveled a good deal, because scholars and rabbis of other cities would beg him to visit them. There is a story that on one of his travels he met a monk at an inn. The Christian was suddenly taken very sick and there was no doctor nearby. The rabbi, who knew something of medicine, took care of the monk, sitting with him day and night and nursing him until he was well.

When the monk was better, he thanked the rabbi and asked, "What can I do to repay you, a Jew who has saved a Christian?" The rabbi said "You owe me nothing. We may not have the same religion, but both of our religions teach us charity. Indeed, in the Jewish religion, charity is a duty. If you should ever come upon a Jew who is in need, help him as I have helped you."

A legend tells us that many years later Rashi traveled to the city of Prague, a city that was far from his home. He was so famous that even the Jews on the other side of Germany had heard of him and begged him to come to visit them and their synagogue, about which you will hear later on.

But bad times for the Jews had already begun in that country, and suddenly there would be attacks on the Jews by ignorant rowdies. An attack of this kind happened while Rashi was in Prague; in the confusion, Rashi was

Rashi and the sick monk

159

taken and put into prison. The most important of all the Christian priests, the bishop, came to visit him there, for the bishop had heard that a famous rabbi was among the prisoners. When the bishop saw Rashi, he fell on his neck and embraced him, for the bishop was the same priest that Rashi had saved years before in the inn.

He asked what he could do for Rashi besides giving him his freedom, and Rashi asked the bishop to stop the attacks on the Jews of the ghetto, where all the Jews of Prague had to live. The bishop gave orders that the Jews should be left in peace, and be protected from the rowdies.

Rashi came home from his travels. He did not have a son to carry on his work, but he had three daughters, and each of them married a scholar. They helped him to answer the many letters that were sent with questions about the Bible and the Talmud, and some of their sons also became famous scholars.

The time of the crusades

One of these grandsons of Rashi wrote hymns and poems as well as commentaries. His name was Jacob Tam. He lived in the time of the Crusades, when Jews were in great danger from soldiers who were on their way across Europe to capture Palestine. You will learn something about them. At one time, Jacob Tam's house was attacked, but he escaped with his life and with what was always most precious to the Jews, his books. We know how precious the books were because of a saying of Rashi and his grandsons, "A drop of ink is worth more than a piece of gold."

THINKING ABOUT WHAT YOU HAVE LEARNED

1. How did Rabbi Solomon ben Isaac get the name Rashi?
2. Why is Rashi remembered as one of the most famous of all Rabbis?

PARENTS

1. Ask your parents why wine is used in holiday celebrations and why there is a Hebrew blessing for wine at all these times.
2. What would be some good questions to be used for an examination for this year's work so far?

An old synagogue

CHAPTER XXVII

How the Synagogue kept Jews together

YOU HAVE BEEN LEARNING how, when the Jews lost their own land, they spread out and settled among different people in many lands. They settled in Spain and in Italy, in France and in Germany and in England. They carried their Torah with them and they built synagogues for study and for worship. So they could stay together. As new things happened in their lives, their wise rabbis wrote more explanations of the Torah and of our Talmud, which is like an encyclopedia. This encyclopedia was written in Palestine and in Babylonia, in what are known as the Dark Ages, although through the Dark Ages our lamp of learning did not go out.

Then came the Middle Ages, and during that time many scholarly rabbis kept adding their commentaries around the pages of the Talmud, until at last the greatest commentaries were finished and the Talmud was printed with their commentaries around each page.

The religious wars

Now you are to learn about another kind of trouble that happened to our people, a bad period through which they lived. This was a time of centuries of religious wars.

You know that there are several great religions in the world, and that in each of the great religions people try to come to understand God. All the great religions teach peace, but each religion takes time to grow, and to become more perfect. During that time, in the history of religion, people have fought and killed others who did not believe as they believed.

Jews have suffered from this, and the time you will study now was such a time.

Today, we live in a land where there is religious freedom, and people are free to worship in their own way. But we must remember that in almost every nation long ago there was only one religion. People were not allowed to worship in another religion. And there are still countries of that kind.

You remember that when the Greeks conquered Judea, they tried to make Jews worship Greek gods. You remember that the first war for religious free-

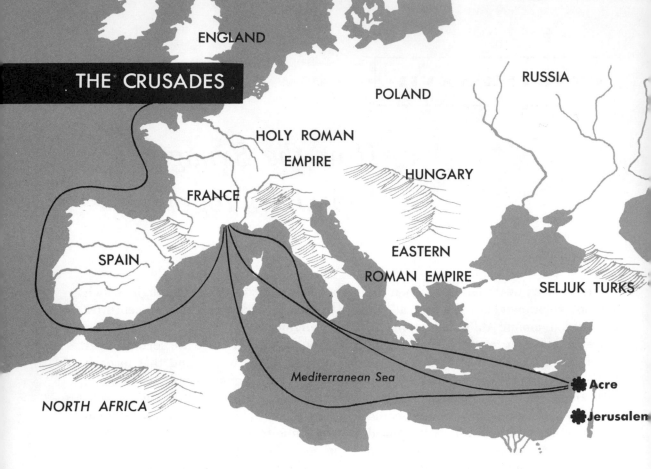

ENGLAND

RUSSIA

POLAND

HOLY ROMAN

EMPIRE

HUNGARY

FRANCE

SPAIN

EASTERN

ROMAN EMPIRE

SELJUK TURKS

NORTH AFRICA

Mediterranean Sea

Acre

Jerusalem

dom was fought against them by the Maccabees, so the Jews could worship the One God, as they knew Him, in their Temple and in their synagogues. That was one kind of religious war, of which we may be proud. It is a war in which people fight for their own faith, for themselves.

But there is another kind of religious war. It is a war in which people try to force their religion on others. Some religions have been spread in that way in the past.

And in the past there were nations that drove out from their lands anyone who would not agree to follow their particular religion. This happened to the Jews in many countries in Europe in the Middle Ages.

At one time they were driven from much of France, where scholars like Rashi had lived and worked in the vineyards of wisdom. Then, much later, Jews were allowed to return. In the Middle Ages, they were also driven out of England. Jews were not allowed to live in England for many generations until a very wise Jew, whom you will learn about, proved to the English leaders that Jews were good and useful people, and that they ought to be free to worship in their own way.

Much of the great trouble for the Jews during the Middle Ages arose because of the Crusades. We know that many noble souls fought in the Crusades. We know famous names such as Richard the Lion Hearted, but we must also know that for the Jewish people the Crusades caused great suffering.

Innocent people were hurt

What were the Crusades? The Crusades were wars between the Christians and the Moslems. Then why were the Jews hurt, if they were not taking part in the war? You know that often an innocent person is hurt in the fighting between two others.

But it is also true that in the time of the Crusades many Christians did not understand the Jews or their religion. They hated the Jews because they believed bad things about them, things which they now know to be untrue.

We live among Christians, and know that they are good people. In other lands, Jews live among Moslems, who are good people. And all three religions believe in the One God. You will learn, one day, how the Christian religion and the Moslem religion grew out of the Jewish religion, so the Christians and Moslems, too, believe in the great Commandments that God gave Moses.

The first Christians were Jews. Long ago, in the terrible days when the Romans were destroying the Second Temple, a few Jews believed that the Messiah had come down to earth. They preached their story of a Messiah to non-Jews, and that was how the Christian church started. During the centuries after, it became the church of the lands of Europe. Jews did not believe in this religion, because there was still great suffering in the world. Therefore, the time of the Messiah, when all would be at peace, could not have come.

A few hundred years after the Christian religion was started, an Arab named Mohammed believed that he heard the word of God. He wrote a book called the Koran, and this was the start of the Moslem religion.

For all three religions Jerusalem is and

Crusaders fight to recapture Jerusalem from the Moslems

has been a holy city. For the Jews, it is the place of the Temple. For the Christians, it is the place where Jesus died. For the Moslems, it is the place where Mohammed set foot, in a vision of heaven.

In the Middle Ages, the Moslems ruled Jerusalem, and the Christians wanted to capture it. That was one of the reasons for the Crusades. The Crusaders were soldiers who marched across Europe on their way to the Mediterranean Sea, where they set sail to capture Jerusalem.

On their way across France and Germany, many of the soldiers became excited because they were on their way to war. And as it was a religious war, they attacked people who did not belong to their religion. They attacked Jews who had been living peacefully in their communities in France and Germany for a long time.

The Jews fled. Whole communities of Jews in France and Germany had to flee for their lives. They got into wagons, carrying with them their Torahs and their few possessions, and set out to find a safe place to live. Some also fled on foot.

Why the Jews fled northward

When you have to get out of the way of a dangerous enemy, you go in the opposite direction. So as the Crusaders were marching south, the Jews fled north. And that is how many of them came to settle in Poland, and in Russia.

Until this time, most of the Jews had lived in warm countries. Palestine was warm, like Florida or California. And Babylonia was even hotter, like Mexico. Egypt and Greece and Italy and Spain were warm countries, and France and Germany were not cold.

But when the Jews fled northward, they had to learn to live and dress differently. In Poland, they wore fur hats and long coats and boots. And in Poland, a country of great woods, they built their synagogues from logs, instead of from stone as they had done in other lands. Some of these log synagogues are still standing, and they look like our old-time block houses, for the Jews gathered

An old fortress synagogue in Poland

in them for protection in times of trouble.

As the Jewish community grew in Poland, schools and academies were started. One of the last great places of Jewish learning, before many Jews came to America, was Poland. Later on, you will learn more about the picturesque Jewish villages in Poland, where the whole life of the town was centered around the synagogue. You will read about the lively characters of these towns, in the humorous stories of Sholem Aleichem. You will also learn some of the tales of the miraculous rabbis, called the Chassidim. And you will learn about the Jews of the great cities, such as Warsaw, and of the scholars and rabbis and artists and Jewish leaders who lived there.

But, before the Jewish community grew in Poland, there was another country that was very important for Jews fleeing from trouble. It was the country of a great Jew named Menasseh ben Israel. His country was Holland, and his city was Amsterdam. His family had come there from Spain.

You remember that Spain was a country that had a Golden Age for the Jews. But at the end there was trouble in Spain too. The rulers of Spain decided that only Christians could live in their land. So they told all the Jews they had to become Christians or leave. This was in the year 1492, which happened to be the same year that Columbus discovered America. But of course Jews could not yet leave for America, since there were to be no settlements in America for more than a lifetime afterward.

Holland became a haven for Jews

The Jews of Spain scattered to many countries. Some of them came to Holland, to the city of Amsterdam, where they found the Dutch people kind and understanding. The Jews found that they were free to start synagogues and schools in peace.

When a great synagogue was opened in Amsterdam, the mayor of the city and other officials came as guests, just as they often do to synagogues and temples in America. The Jews who had come to Amsterdam in ships from Spain had brought with them their Torah scrolls. And at the opening of the Amsterdam synagogue there were seventy-seven Torahs, which the fleeing Jews had carried as their most precious possessions. At the ceremony, there were speeches in Hebrew, Dutch, Spanish, Portuguese, Latin, and French.

Among the Jews of Holland were some who knew many languages, because the Jews of Holland had come through many lands. One boy who could read and write in Dutch, Hebrew, Spanish, Latin and Portuguese by the time he was fifteen, was Menasseh ben Israel, the brightest student of the Torah school. His father had been put in prison and tortured in Portugal, because he would not give up the Jewish religion. Then he had escaped with his family to Holland.

Menasseh went to the Torah school and then to the academy, or yeshiva, where he studied the Talmud. When he was seventeen years old, he wrote a Hebrew grammar. When he was twenty years old he became a rabbi of *165* one of the three small synagogues in Amsterdam, before the great synagogue was built.

As rabbis in olden days earned their living at other work, Menasseh ben Israel was a printer. He did the first printing in the Hebrew language in Holland. He also wrote and published books.

One of these books became well known among non-Jews, and Menasseh ben Israel became an important personage in Amsterdam. He was even known in other countries, including England, where Jews were then not allowed to live.

Among the non-Jews in Amsterdam who were friends of Menasseh was the great painter, Rembrandt, and he made a number of etchings of the leader of the Jewish community. We can see what a kindly man Menasseh was from his smiling eyes in the pictures of Rembrandt. The great artist also drew illustrations for one of Menasseh's books.

How the Jews came to live in England

It was one of these books that opened the way for the Jews to return to live in England. Menasseh ben Israel wrote a book about a Jewish belief that the real time of the Messiah, the time of peace, would come when the Jews had been scattered into every country in the whole world. Only then, it was believed, would they again be gathered together to go to the land of Israel.

''The Hope of Israel'' was the name of the book in which Menasseh explained this belief, and a copy of it was sent to the English leader, Oliver Crom-

Rembrandt painting a portrait of Menasseh ben Israel

well. As Cromwell was a Puritan, and a great student of the Bible, he became quite interested in this book. Then Menasseh ben Israel wrote to Cromwell and pointed out that England was the only country where there were no Jews. How could the time of peace, the time of the Messiah come, unless the Jews were living in every country in the world?

America had been discovered by then, and there were Puritan colonies in America, and Menasseh wrote to Cromwell that even in the strange new land of the Indians there were Jews. Cromwell allowed Menasseh ben Israel to come to London to plead that Jews should again be permitted to live in England. Menasseh made him see that Jews were not the strange, dangerous people that they had been believed to be by superstitious folk. He made him see that Jews could help England grow strong in trade. And although Cromwell did not at once grant the petition of the Jew from Holland, it was not many years before Jews were again allowed to live and worship in their own synagogues in England. Since then, the Jewish community in England has become one of the most important in the world.

From the Old World to the New

By that time there were Jews in America, too. Some Jews who came to settle in New York were from Menasseh ben Israel's great city in Holland. For New York was at that time a Dutch city; it was even called New Amsterdam. And the Jewish settlers from Holland had Spanish names, like Mendes, or Gomes, or Pinto. For like Menasseh ben Israel, they were sons of Jews who had fled from Spain.

It was a long way around from Spain to Holland to America. But soon after the Jews arrived, the first synagogue was started in New Amsterdam, and the very same congregation, Shearith Israel, still worships in the city of New York.

Meanwhile, Jews came to America from other countries, too. They came from Germany, from Poland, from Russia, and from many other lands. They did not speak the same language. They studied the same Torah, but not always in exactly the same ways.

For some of them had the ways of Jews who had lived in Spain for hundreds of years. Others had the ways of Jews who had lived in Germany for hundreds of years. Others had the ways of Jews who had lived in Poland and Russia for hundreds of years. But all Jews everywhere believe in God and the prophets, in the Torah, in justice, in Hillel's Golden Rule, and in peace.

The same the world over

No matter what land Jews came from, they brought the same Torah. Their synagogues may have looked different, but to a Jew it is not the walls of the synagogue that are important, but what is inside the walls. And you will see that inside they were very much the same.

In the beginning a synagogue may simply be the front room of someone's house, or the back room, so long as it is a place where ten Jews can pray together. It may be a basement, or even a cave as in the days of Rabbi Akiba and Bar Kochba.

You remember that after the Golden Age in Spain the Spanish Jews were all commanded to become Christians. Those who could, fled from Spain at once. But some could not get away, and became secret Jews. They had secret synagogues in caves, in their cellars, or in secret rooms in their homes. Their children were secretly taught the Torah. Their scrolls were kept hidden.

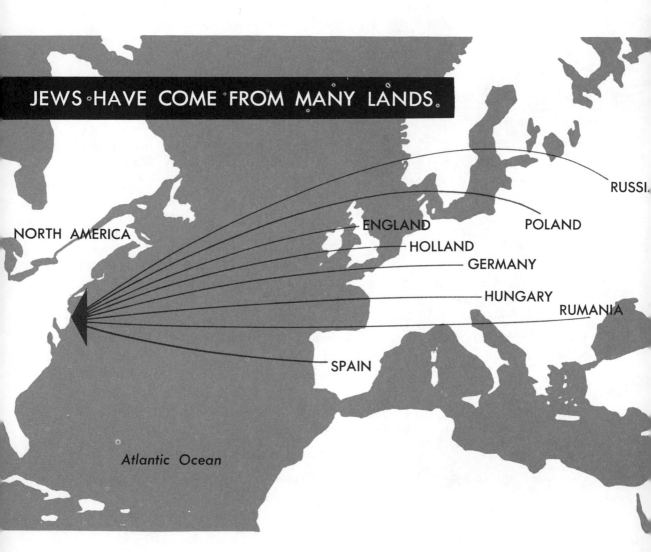

JEWS·HAVE COME·FROM MANY LANDS.

RUSSI.
POLAND
ENGLAND
HOLLAND
GERMANY
NORTH AMERICA
HUNGARY
RUMANIA
SPAIN

Atlantic Ocean

As soon as possible, they too fled from Spain. And after living for a time in other lands, such as Holland, some of them wanted to try the new world, and they came to America. Over three hundred years ago the first group of Spanish Jews started a synagogue here. Our records tell us that is was upstairs over a store, and some years afterward a building was put up for this congregation and its school. Through the years, the same congregation moved, each time to a larger and more beautiful synagogue. But many of the old customs and rituals of the Spanish Jews were kept up by this historic congregation. In the synagogue of the Spanish Jews the Bimah is in the middle of the sanctuary instead of at the far end, so that the Torah is carried ceremoniously from the Ark at the far end, to the Bimah in the center, each time it is opened to be read.

Next to the Spanish Jews, some of the oldest congregations in America are those of the German Jews. There were many changes of custom among the German Jews when the Reform synagogues became popular. These were synagogues where men and women sat together, instead of sitting in separate parts of the hall. The men did not always wear hats. And only part of the service was in Hebrew, the rest was in German or English.

Not all German synagogues were Reform. Some were Orthodox, or Conservative.

The third great group of Jews who came were from Poland and Russia, and other Eastern European countries such as Hungary and Romania. They were mostly Orthodox. Some of them believed in keeping the same kind of clothes they had worn in the old country, the long coats, and the large black hats. They kept their side-curls that grew along their cheeks, and they often had beautiful long beards.

But no matter what differences there might be, the main things were the same in every synagogue. There was the Ark, with the scrolls. And the Eternal Light. And the Torah prayers. And the Sabbath. And the holidays.

Thus, no matter how many lands they lived in, and how many centuries they were separated from each other, when Jews came together again the most important things in their lives were the same.

THINKING ABOUT WHAT YOU HAVE LEARNED

1. In what way is Jerusalem holy to three religions?
2. How did Menasseh ben Israel try to convince Oliver Cromwell that the Messiah would come if Jews would be allowed to return to England?

PARENTS

1. How do Jews today feel about convincing other people to change their religion to Judaism?
2. Are there countries today where Jews wish to leave and are being helped by Jews in other lands to settle in new homes?

CHAPTER XXVIII

How Jews worship all around the world

WHEN THE SAGE OF Amsterdam, Menasseh ben Israel, went to London to ask that the Jews be allowed to come back and live in England, you remember that he told Oliver Cromwell a prophecy. He said that the time of peace could not come until Jews lived in every country in the world. We do not know God's way, so we do not know when the great time of peace that we call the time of the Messiah will truly come. Perhaps it will come little by little as the people of the world truly seek for peace. Perhaps the meaning of the prophecy was that when any people are allowed to dwell freely among any other people, as the Jews might dwell freely in all the world, this in itself would be a sign. It would be a sign that the people of the world had learned the lesson of not doing to others what you would not have them do to you.

Whatever we think of the prophecy, it is true that Jews live in virtually every country in the world, and wherever they live, they have their synagogues. And as we visit some of their synagogues, we can see how some

are ancient and some are new, but all contain the Torah.

If we were to take a trip around the the world, we would find these synagogues in every land. We would find synagogues in every large city of Europe, Asia, and Africa, in Australia, and South America. You know about some of these synagogues that have been part of our history. You have learned about synagogues in America, and in Babylonia, Spain, France, Germany, Poland, and Holland.

Many of the synagogues in the famous cities of Europe, in London, Paris, and Berlin, are very much like our own, because they were built in the past few hundred years. Now, however, we will examine some unusual synagogues, in a trip around the world.

The legend of the Golem

We may begin in a wondrous synagogue that has a legend. It is in the city of Prague, in Czechoslovakia. You will remember the tale of one of our great scholars, Rashi, who traveled from France as far as Prague, and how there was trouble in the ghetto of Prague, but Rashi was saved.

In those countries, a few centuries ago, there were rowdies who would attack the Jews. You remember that some of their synagogues were built like block-houses, for protection. And there are other stories of how the Jews were protected. One is about the famous old synagogue in Prague. It is a legend about a great rabbi, who could perform miracles. He dreamed of protecting his people against their attackers.

And the legend tells us that this rabbi went up into the attic of the ancient synagogue, and made a giant statue out of clay. The statue was called the Golem. And in times of trouble, the legend tells us, the giant Golem would come to life and go out and protect the Jews against the rowdies.

Perhaps the meaning of this is that our greatest strength is in our faith in the synagogue, and that this faith, like a giant, can protect us.

The famous synagogue of this legend still stands in the city of Prague. It is called the Alt-Neu Shul, meaning the Old-New synagogue, because parts of it were built in different centuries.

The old part is said to be so old that some people believe it was built with stones brought by Jews from Palestine, when the Second Temple was destroyed. But we know that the synagogue was actually built seven hundred years ago, long after the destruction of the Temple.

South to the heart of Africa

Perhaps the Jews first came to Prague from the south, from Budapest, which is nearer to Palestine, where they started. We know that there were Jews in Budapest nearly two thousand years ago, when the Second Temple was destroyed. The Jews of that time must have had a synagogue, but there are no records of it. However, there are records of a synagogue from the year

The Golem — the clay giant of Prague

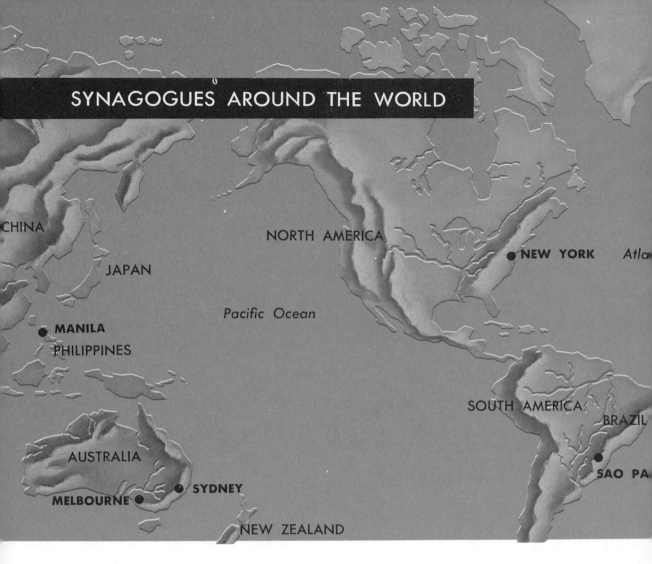

CHINA

NORTH AMERICA

NEW YORK Atla

JAPAN

Pacific Ocean

MANILA

PHILIPPINES

SOUTH AMERICA

BRAZIL

AUSTRALIA

SAO PA

SYDNEY

MELBOURNE

NEW ZEALAND

1100. Some of the finest synagogues of modern times were built in Budapest. One of them was the Great Synagogue in Dohany Street.

If we keep going back, southward, we come to Salonika, a very ancient seaport which the Jews could reach from Palestine. It may have been one of their first stops in their travels. We know that there was a synagogue in Salonika over two thousand years ago. For even before the fall of the Temple,

Jewish traders, sailing around the Mediterranean Sea, must have started a community in this port.

Across the sea from Salonika is Damascus, in the land of Syria. This is a land that we have heard about from the earliest times of the Jews. You remember that Alexander the Great, who conquered so many of the countries around the Mediterranean Sea, started his conquests in Syria.

The oldest city in Syria, Damascus,

172

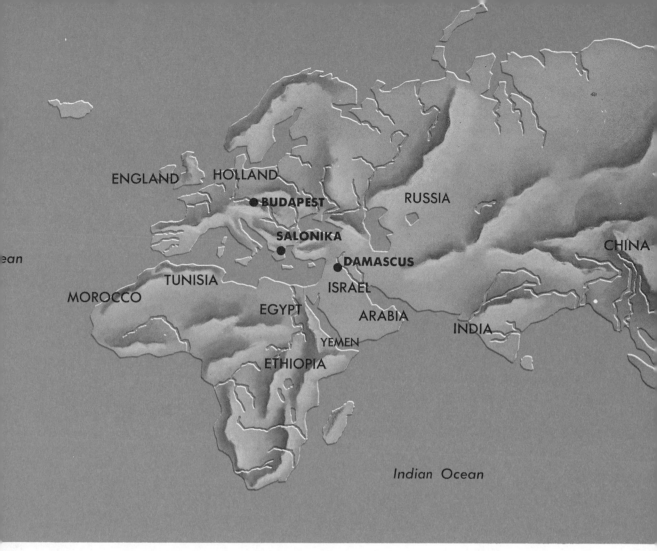

ENGLAND HOLLAND

RUSSIA

●BUDAPEST

SALONIKA

DAMASCUS

CHINA

ean

TUNISIA

ISRAEL

MOROCCO

EGYPT

ARABIA

INDIA

YEMEN

ETHIOPIA

Indian Ocean

is mentioned many times in the Bible. And the synagogues of Damascus are the oldest in the world. In Syria is Dura-Europos, where the ancient synagogue paintings were found.

From Syria we might travel past many lands where Jews have lived from ancient times. We might travel down to the heart of Africa, to Ethiopia where the Jews are black-skinned. They live in remote villages, and they believe they are descended from King Solomon and the Queen of Sheba. They may worship in their huts or even in tents, bringing us back to very early times.

East to Japan

From Africa we could cross the Red Sea to the bottom of Arabia, and there, too, in the land of Yemen, ancient Jewish tribes believed they were descended from Solomon's times. Almost all of the Yemenites have now gone to live in Israel. From Yemen you could sail 173 across the Arabian Sea and come to India.

The Jews of India say that their ancestors came not by sea but by caravan routes across the Arabian deserts in the old, old days, before the Second Temple. They came in the time of the First Temple, in the time of King Solomon. These Jews call themselves the B'nai Israel, the children of Israel. And there is a strange kind of proof that their community comes from the days of King Solomon. The proof is that they do not celebrate Hanukah among their holidays.

You know that Hanukah celebrates the victory of the Maccabees, which came hundreds of years after the time of King Solomon. So if the B'nai Israel keep their holidays as they did in the very old times, and if they do not keep Hanukah, it may indeed show that their community is clinging to the ways that were started before the time of the Maccabees.

There are other Jewish communities in India, for in modern times Jews have come to settle in all the large cities of many lands. But the B'nai Israel have kept many of their very ancient customs.

If we keep traveling eastward, eventually we will reach China. Just as with India, there were Jewish traders who went to China even during the ancient times of the First Temple. There is a legend about a ship that was sent by King Solomon to trade with the Chinese, in "the land of silk." And from the Middle Ages, there are the remains of a synagogue at Kai Fung Foo, records showing that it was built in 1160, with

the aid of the Chinese Emperor.

From China we cross the water to Japan. And here we find a strange story about the Jews. Not too long ago, Japan was a closed country ruled by an emperor; no foreigners could enter Japan. But then things changed, and people from Europe and America came to do business with the Japanese. When they first came to this closed country they were puzzled, for they found that many places had names similar to names in the Bible. They also found some Japanese customs very much like the customs described in the Bible. How could these Biblical names and customs have come to this faraway, closed country?

One answer that has been given is that the Japanese might be descendants of the Ten Lost Tribes that were driven out of Israel by the ancient Assyrians. Some scholars believe the tribes may have wandered eastward and even reached Japan. But we do not know

whether this is really so.

In modern times, Jews came to Japan from Russia and from other countries. The synagogue in Nagasaki was built in 1889 by Jews from Russia.

Across the wide Pacific

Now if we start back across the Pacific Ocean, we will have traveled almost around the world! In the Pacific are the islands of the Philippines. These islands were discovered by Spanish explorers, so it is no surprise that some of the first settlers were secret Jews of Spain called Marranos.

But later, other Jews came to the Philippines. In 1840, a group of German Jews arrived. And the Jewish community grew. This community built a new temple, the Emile Temple, in 1924 in Manila.

If we turn south in the Pacific Ocean, we come to the country that is said to be "way down under." This is Australia. It is a new country, even newer than America.

It has been settled by Englishmen. Jews came, too, in 1617, and helped to build up this new country.

The largest Jewish community in Australia is in the city of Sydney. Its synagogue was built in 1844. The second largest Jewish community is in Melbourne.

From the far Pacific lands of Australia and New Zealand, where some of the newest Jewish communities exist, you could sail to America.

Completing the circle

You know when the Jews came to North America. They came to South America, too. One of their oldest settlements in South America is in Sao Paulo, a seaport of Brazil. The Jewish community of Sao Paulo was started by the secret Jews of Spain, the Marranos. They were some of the same Jews who

A synagogue in the Far East

came to New Amsterdam, or New York, and to the Philippines, so you see that many of us may have distant relatives in other parts of the world.

If we keep sailing from South America, on the last lap of a cruise around the world, we come to Africa. And along the upper part of Africa, we may pass by way of the Atlas mountains, where Jews have lived in caves from ancient times to this day.

And from these lands, Morocco and Tunisia, we come into Egypt, the land of the stories of Joseph, and of Moses. There are very old Jewish families living in Egypt, and there are very old synagogues, where some of our most important ancient scrolls have been discovered. They were found by Professor Solomon Schechter in the storehouse of a synagogue that had a very long history. It went back not only to the Middle Ages but to the Dark Ages. And these manuscripts tell us much about the fate of the Jews after the fall of the Temple, when they began to be scattered over the world.

From Egypt, we may follow the path of Moses to Israel. And just as the Jews were once scattered, many of them are now returning from all parts of the world. In modern Israel there are Jews from seventy different countries. There are Jews who once worshipped in the synagogue in Prague, there are Jews from Budapest and ancient Salonika. There are Jews from India, and even from China. There are Jews from Australia and America. There are black-skinned Jews from Ethiopia, and brown-skinned Jews from Egypt. And they have all brought their Torahs back to Israel.

And thus, our history, starting from ancient times, and growing and moving from country to country, has come full circle, around the world and back.

THINKING ABOUT WHAT YOU HAVE LEARNED

1. What makes us think that the Jews came to India before the Maccabees fought their war for religious freedom?
2. Why did the Rabbi of Prague make a Golem?

PARENTS

1. Have your parents or any of their friends visited synagogues in foreign countries?
2. Why is it important to know that there are synagogues in India, China, Japan, Ethiopia and other lands around the world?

Jewish traders in frontier America

The Synagogue and you

CHAPTER XXIX

The chain of learning

Now YOU KNOW ALMOST the whole story of the synagogue. Perhaps when you began you thought, why, everybody can see all there is to know about a synagogue. It is a building where we worship, and go to religious school. You know that even the building is not always the same. Some may be round, some tall; some may be old synagogues without windows, or new synagogues with walls of glass; and some may be built like pagodas, and some like schools. But in all of them there is Jewish worship and Jewish learning. In the story of our worship, we started with your own synagogue and then we went far back to learn about the oldest synagogues of all, in all the world. And you learned about worship, even before

there was a synagogue with a roof on it.

You learned about Abraham worshipping on stone altars. And about Moses gathering the people together to tell them God's law. That was a kind of open-air synagogue. Then you learned about Moses having a tent built for the Ark, and for the tablets of the Ten Commandments — a tent for the Holy of Holies. That was the earliest kind of synagogue.

You learned that in those ancient places of worship, the priests held the service. But you also learned that over the centuries it became the people themselves who performed the service.

You learned that when the Temple of King Solomon, in Jerusalem, was destroyed, the Jews were taken to Baby-

lonia, and as they had no temple there, the scribes helped them to read and to recite the Scriptures. That was the beginning of our own kind of worship, in which everyone takes part.

You learned that when the Jews went from Babylonia back to Jerusalem, Ezra the Scribe stood on a platform at the water gate and read the Scriptures to the people. You learned that after we built the Second Temple, we also built synagogues in Jerusalem, and in all the towns and villages. We started schools in the synagogues, just as we have them today.

And you learned that when the Second Temple was destroyed by the Roman soldiers, the Jews continued to study their Torah in their schools and colleges, and that was what kept them together.

You learned that when the Jews were again driven out of Palestine, they carried their Torahs with them. And instead of losing their laws, they worked to make them more perfect, in all the countries where they went.

You learned that great Jewish scholars went back and forth from one country to another, to keep the colleges at their best. Some went back to Baby-

lonia; they created a great work called the Talmud. Other scholars in Jerusalem also put together a Talmud. When times became bad in Babylonia, the great scholars moved to Spain, and the Golden Age of Jewish learning took place in Spain. Other Jews moved to France and to Germany. When the Crusaders burned Jewish books and synagogues in those lands, the Jews put their children and their Torahs in their wagons and fled to Poland and to Russia.

Meanwhile, the Golden Age came to an end in Spain. When the rulers and Inquisitors tried to make the Jews give up their religion, the Jews took their Torahs and their Talmuds, placed their families in boats, and sailed to different parts of the world. Some went to Amsterdam, and some came from Amsterdam to South America and to North America.

Years later, when times grew bad in Poland and Russia, and there were attacks upon the Jews, many of them took their families and their scrolls, their Torahs and their scholarly works, and came to America. Some of us may have had grandparents among them.

Schools were built here, and also colleges for higher Jewish studies. Much

The story of Judaism: from Abraham to the New World

179

of the great learning that had once been carried on in Palestine, and in Babylonia, and in Spain, and in Amsterdam, and in Vilna, in Poland, was now carried on in the United States.

Then there was a world war. And this was the greatest tragedy for those Jews who still lived in Europe. For Hitler tried to kill all the Jews. Numbers of them escaped to Palestine. After the war, the Jews of Palestine created Israel as a free nation again, and Jews from many lands returned to live there.

Just as in the days of Ezra, the first thought of the Jews who went back to Israel was to start schools and colleges, universities and centers of Jewish learning. Some of these are modern colleges where every kind of subject is studied. And some, called Yeshivoth, continue the work of the old synagogue schools, in the religious study of the Talmud.

From then till now

Now our best scholars may go back and forth from America to Israel and from Israel to America, to keep alive our knowledge of Jewish law, literature, customs, and history. Our most learned rabbis of today may visit Jerusalem to hold discussions with the rabbis there. We ourselves may one day visit Israel to see the land of the Torah.

So you see that our history has a road that winds all over the world. And on this road are the many places where Jews have lived, sometimes for hundreds of years. In the life of a people, a hundred years is the same as a day in the life of a person.

And these many places all have syna-gogues that the Jews built along the winding road of their history.

Indeed, when a Jew travels and finds himself in a strange city or a strange land, often the first thing he will do will be to seek the synagogue, not only if he wishes to pray, but because he knows that through it he will be able to find friends, and to find help if he needs help. And in the synagogue he will find things to interest his mind, for he will meet people who have had an education similar to the one he has had.

Study is never finished

You have seen how Moses and the other prophets brought us the Torah of God.

And how Ezra and the other scribes wrote down this Torah and started our synagogues.

The great sages from Hillel to Judah HaNasi put together all the laws that grew around the Torah. This was the Mishnah.

The rabbis in Palestine and in Babylonia gathered all the explanations and stories about the Mishnah. And this became the Talmud.

Then the Jews of Spain, like Maimonides, picked out the main beliefs from the vast Talmud, so that all Jews could have them in an orderly form.

The Jews of France and Germany, like Rashi, wrote Commentaries, or discussions of the Talmud, for our scholars.

And wherever Jews went in the world, they carried their Torah and all the wisdom that grew out of it.

So you see that out of the Tablets grew the Torah. And out of the Torah

Clay tablets to the printed book

grew the Mishnah laws. And from the Mishnah grew the Talmud. And around the Talmud were written the Commentaries.

Of course, every Jew cannot be expected to learn all that is in these books. But our people have always believed that the study of the Torah is never finished. Each person should learn as much as he can; he should keep studying and reading our books, all his life.

Many people read the Bible over and over because it is so interesting. There are so many wonderful stories in it. New, deeper thoughts are always coming to us from it. Modern writers are always writing whole new books out of the Torah stories; they tell the story of David, or of Joseph, or of Ruth, or of Esther, again and again. But somehow these stories are not as beautiful as they are in the first scrolls.

You remember how even far back in the Babylonian days the grown-ups had classes for adults, called the Kallah. Today, too, our synagogues have classes for boys and girls who have finished their Bar Mitzvah and their Bas Mitzvah. They can then go on and study for Confirmation. And after they have had their Confirmation, they can go on with Bible study classes, and Hebrew classes, and all kinds of Jewish studies for grown-ups.

Some boys and girls when they grow up become so interested in their Jewish studies that they want to make this their life work. They want to become teachers of Hebrew, or rabbis. Even if they decide to have another profession, they may want to teach in a synagogue   *181* school, such as this, as part of their work.

For those who want to become rabbis, or Jewish community workers, we have special schools, just as there are special schools for doctors and lawyers and artists and engineers.

The most important Jewish colleges are those that train rabbis. We have a number of them in America, just as there were in Babylonia, and in Spain, and in Poland, and just as there were and still are in Jerusalem.

These colleges for rabbis and Jewish leaders carry on the work that was begun by the great rabbis over two thousand years ago. The rabbis and Jewish leaders study in order to guide you as you grow up, and to help you through your life as a Jew.

Thus, all this knowledge, all these laws, through the ages, through all the lands, have been kept for you. Your rabbi and your teachers have held meetings with your parents and other parents of the congregation in order to arrange this school in which you are now studying. They have tried to make it a good school and an interesting one, and also a school in which you will feel happy.

So the chain of knowledge has come down to you. The synagogue for you has been a house of study, as well as a house of worship. Though you may have Purim and Hanukah parties, and social activities, and many enjoyable times here, you do not forget that the school is the main part of the synagogue made especially for you, to prepare you for your manhood and womanhood in the congregation.

Let us see how you will take part in the congregation, later on.

THINKING ABOUT WHAT YOU HAVE LEARNED

1. Who are five of the most important heroes in the story of worship from the beginning to the present day?
2. How does your congregation help training schools from which your Rabbi, Cantor, or Educational Director graduated? How can your class help?

PARENTS

1. Ask your parents if they would agree with your choice of the five heroes of worship?
2. What would help a boy today decide if he wanted to become a Rabbi, a Cantor, or an Educational Director?

CHAPTER XXX

When you become a member of a Synagogue

Now you know a good deal about the synagogue. At every age in your life, the doors of the synagogue will be open for you. The mothers and fathers in the congregation, and the rabbi, and the whole Jewish community, have made sure that the synagogue is here for you. Even the whole Jewish people of the past have taken care that it would be here for you.

A house of study

What has the synagogue been for you until now? You have come here mostly for your religious study. So it has been a house of study for you; in Hebrew the name would be Beth Hamidrash. And that is one of the names by which the synagogue has been called, in all the ages. In the old days, the religious schools were the only schools. All that children learned, they learned there. But now we have divided up our subjects, and we study the Jewish subjects in this school. We study the Bible and Jewish history and literature. We will study Jewish customs and ceremonies, and

worship, and Jewish life. We can learn the Hebrew language. We can go on learning more about the Jews, all our lives. Therefore, this is a house of study.

The synagogue is a house of study

But the synagogue is also called by two other names. Let us see about their meaning.

A house of gathering

Perhaps the very first of the three names of the synagogues was Beth Haknesseth. This means the house of gathering, the place where the people come together to meet for all things, for worship, for discussions, and for celebrations.

You may read in the papers that the name of the Congress in Israel is Knesseth. Of course it is not a synagogue. But this name reminds us that the gathering of the people, the coming together, is part of our tradition. So you see that the idea of democracy, the idea of deciding things through a meeting of the people, is a very old idea with the Jews. It is so old, among our people, that it

has given us one of the names of the synagogue.

Already, you may belong to a children's club in the synagogue. You may discuss all kinds of problems, and you may vote. And as you grow older, you will come to many gatherings of all kinds in the synagogue.

When you are going to high school, you can join a youth group that may meet in the synagogue, and besides coming to study, you may find many activities. Some temples have youth groups that hold dances, or organize their own choral group. There are socials, and teams for different sports, and square dances, and dramatic clubs.

The youth groups may visit other religious groups in inter-faith meetings, and may explain our faith to their non-Jewish friends. They may become ushers, and help out at bazaars and at other grown-up activities.

Soon you may find yourself in a college group, with lecture forums, formal dances, and perhaps your own special holiday parties. And of course you will still have all the other activities, such as sports and dramatics and singing.

Then comes the young adults' group, which may have special study clubs for reading the best Jewish books and for listening to music. They may have discussion meetings about religious customs. They may have parties, and folk dancing, and classes where they discuss our ideas about marriage.

When you get married, you can join the young couples' group, and have parties at each other's homes, and talk about current affairs. By then you will have found your own favorite activities in the synagogue—music, teaching, volunteering to help raise funds for important Jewish institutions, or interfaith work.

You will come to meetings of the congregation and vote on how to run the synagogue..

Then you may join the special clubs for men and women, the Brotherhood or the Sisterhood. The men may have Sunday breakfast meetings for synagogue affairs, or to hear famous speakers, or to hear about Jews in other lands. Men and women may join the Community Council as representatives of the synagogue, to meet with church people and others. Men usually take care of the finances of the synagogue. They may be elected as officers of the synagogue. And they may give their time to youth groups, to coaching sports, or to singing.

The women will do many of the things the men do, but they will also have special activities, like sewing groups, or bazaars, or a book and gift shop. They may have a group to discuss family education. They may volunteer to bake cakes or to make decorations for parties at the synagogue.

As you grow older, no matter which activities you choose, or how many activities you choose, you will remember the synagogue as three things: a house of study, a house of gathering, and a house of prayer.

Selling toys at a synagogue bazaar

A house of worship

The third name for the synagogue is Beth Hatifila, which means the house of prayer. You may already take part in prayer in the children's services, or you may sit with the adults. Soon you may be Bar Mitzvah; perhaps you will be confirmed. Always in Sabbath services and on the holidays, the synagogue will be a Beth Hatifila for you. You will come to the synagogue to pray whenever you feel in need of prayer.

Even before the synagogue was a house of study or a house of gathering, it was a house of prayer. For we are told this in the wise sayings of our great rabbis, which show us how much the synagogue meant to our fathers and to our father's fathers.

About going to the synagogue: The Bible says, "Abraham rose early in the morning and went to the place where he stood before the Lord."

Long ago, as we know, our sage, Rabbi Hillel, said: "Do not separate thyself from thy community." In this way he told us that man should never live only for himself. He knew that each person belonged with the community, not only to keep from being selfish, but to keep well and happy.

You may say, "But of course. Every child knows that." And it is true that we sometimes know things as children that we forget when we grow up. Children like to play and work together. Of course there are also times when children and grown-ups like and need to be alone with their thoughts, and with their work, and with their pleasure. But we know that people who are separated from their community can become unhappy.

To take part in the community is really a part of our human nature. You are taking part in the community through this school. You came to study, to meet with your friends and to worship with them. And this means you will be well prepared to take part in the Jewish community as you grow up. And you can take part all your life, through the synagogue.

So, for you, the story of the synagogue has just begun.

THINKING ABOUT WHAT YOU HAVE LEARNED

1. Do you remember the three names of the synagogue in Hebrew?
2. Which activities of your synagogue would be of greatest interest to a new member?

PARENTS

1. Ask your parents to help you write a letter to the authors of this book telling them what you enjoyed and what ideas you have for making it better.

Index